I0117723

LEGITIMATE PREFERENCE

TIM VORGENS

LEGITIMATE PREFERENCE

RECLAIMING THE RIGHT TO ONE'S OWN

ARKTOS

LONDON 2025

ΛRKTOS

🌐 Arktos.com 📘 fb.com/Arktos ▶ 📷 arktosmedia ✖ arktosjournal

Copyright © 2025 by Arktos Media Ltd.

All rights reserved. No part of this book may be reproduced or utilised in any form or by any means (whether electronic or mechanical), including photocopying, recording or by any information storage and retrieval system, without permission in writing from the publisher.

ISBN

978-1-917646-91-8 (Paperback)

978-1-917646-92-5 (Hardback)

978-1-917646-93-2 (Ebook)

Editing

Jafe Arnold

Layout and Cover

Tor Westman

CONTENTS

Foreword by Jared Taylor

As I write these lines, France is in turmoil over a proposed pension reform that would raise the retirement age from 62 to 64. Public transport is paralyzed, schools are disrupted, garbage piles up in the streets, gas stations run dry. The French can indeed rise up against their rulers whenever they choose — and I admire that spirit.

Yet, as a foreigner, I am puzzled. With life expectancy rising and the number of working-age Frenchmen shrinking, is it truly scandalous to propose a gradual increase in the retirement age? Of course, it is for the French to decide. But are there not other issues that deserve at least as much national mobilization?

I have lived and studied in France. I deeply admire the French — their magnificent culture, their heroic and tragic history, the innumerable gifts they have made to world civilization, their hopes and limitless potential. I believe that, by virtue of its greatness alone, France has a duty not only to itself but also to the world: to remain faithful to its heritage and to work toward a future worthy of its past.

For that to happen, it is obvious that France must remain proudly French. How could a France turned Afro-Islamic-Asian and polyglot — what Tim Vorgens aptly calls a "former France" — still be the France of Vercingetorix, of Molière, of Pascal, of Victor Hugo, of Debussy, or of Claudie Haigneré? That is why today's upheaval in France strikes me as strangely misplaced.

What Vorgens calls *Legitimate Preference* is infinitely more important than any shift in the retirement age. For White Frenchmen, and for Whites everywhere, the right to say, "Yes, we prefer our own," ought to be a matter of national policy. And it should be the cause of a vast popular mobilization.

The aspirations of the French, like those of nearly all Westerners, have been perverted. What drives them today is the hope of personal gratification rather than the prospect of regained national greatness. My own nation is no different — indeed, it is worse. Americans pioneered every form of intellectual trickery and emotional blackmail used to subvert Legitimate Preference.

This is why, as an American, I so warmly welcome Mr. Vorgens's book. It speaks to all of us, to the entire European brotherhood of which Americans — together with Canadians, Australians, New Zealanders, and Afrikaners — are a part. We are united in the same struggle: to ensure the survival and prosperity of our besieged people.

This book contains many striking ideas and observations. I will comment on only a few. One is especially important for someone like me, who has spent decades writing and speaking on behalf of our people. Vorgens tells us that logic alone is doomed to fail. That is a bitter lesson I have had to learn again and again. As he writes, "Truth by itself has no power," and "The rationality of our cause is probably not enough."

For those of us who openly declare our love for our people, nothing seems more self-evident than Legitimate Preference. Yet, as Mr. Vorgens explains, "Only a rational fanaticism — a fanaticism of thought able to wield the full emotional spectrum of political marketing — can compete with the Left and defeat it." If we advance only logical arguments, we cannot win. As Vorgens suggests, if a man is so corrupted that he does not prefer his own children — or his own people — you cannot persuade him with syllogisms. That love must be awakened through the entire range of human emotion.

I believe, with Vorgens, that deep in the European soul lies a dormant love for our people. It is a hard lesson, but he is right: "The reasonable Right is never heard. Society listens only to the shouts, not to the wise voices." We who would be wise must learn to shout — not as our enemies do, but with the eloquent anguish of the truly besieged. We must also rouse our people by leadership by example, by striving always to embody the nobility we have inherited from our ancestors.

Ultimately, Vorgens's aspirations must also be those of France itself: "As long as the state is not reclaimed by preferential logic and put at the service of a Preferist society, resources will be distributed illegitimately."

We Europeans live under regimes that claim to represent us but in truth betray us. When the French take to the streets, don yellow vests, or call for votes of no confidence, it is to demand genuine representation.

That day has not yet come. It will come only if the minority among us who clearly see their duty can draw the essential lessons of this book. As Vorgens writes, Legitimate Preference must become for us "a kind of inner law" — a law so natural that "an unapologetically Preferist life will taste of innocence and serenity."

Only when a substantial number of us can be radical dissidents while still carrying "the taste of innocence and serenity" will we have a movement that stands on the path to success.

Finally, Vorgens reminds us that our duty to our ancestors and our obligation to generations yet unborn is not only to preserve past achievements: "A greater capacity for Legitimate Preference is the condition for Europeans to one day produce the overman Nietzsche longed for, the *Homo Prometheus*."

Our people have been great. If we act as we must, they can be greater still.

JARED TAYLOR
Oakton, Virginia
March 20, 2023

Author's Preface

THIS BOOK tackles a seemingly banal subject from what may be a more original angle: the right of Whites to shape their own destiny, by claiming the right to prefer themselves. It brings together different texts written since 2019 and denounces the abuse of the egalitarian argument that forces Whites to love what they do not love and to live alongside those who replace them. It also examines the methods by which this right to *Legitimate Preference* can be won. In a sense, it is a book of law — written by someone wholly incompetent in that field.

Marcel Duchamp had this written on his gravestone: *"It is always the others who die."* That is true for individuals. But genetic and civilizational families die as well. And when they do, it is *we* who die. Science tells us that death is a process. Medicine shows that it is sometimes reversible — given the right methods and the will to save what can still be saved. Even in dying societies there are healthy parts. Those healthy parts must form communities, to become new organisms that will live on.

This book is addressed to the healthy parts.

The Left's conspiracy-mongering — which criminalizes even noticing the Great Replacement — has a stupid and criminal purpose: to put Whites in danger, simply for the cheap honor of being elected "the most moral community in the world." This de-vitalized segment of society clings to the pseudo-science that human races do not exist, and forces us into a pseudo-society where our rights as natives no longer exist. It drains our strength, invites the enemy to our table, denies reality, sells hypnosis, and runs off with the cashbox.

In order to claim rights, you need an intolerable situation and concepts forged for combat. That is exactly where we are.

Until Elon Musk buys back the West, *Legitimate Preference* can rally the healthy parts and distribute the antidote.

I want naïve Europeans to recover their rights as native Europeans. If you oppose this, you are the enemy.

WARNING!

The following work contains formulations that may offend the sensibilities of some readers. It is in no way intended to encourage offensive or disrespectful behavior toward anyone. It merely describes a feeling of Preference and suggests cultivating this attitude inwardly.

Did You Say "Legitimate Preference"?

THERE EXISTS a genetic-cultural group from which we once emerged, a group without which neither our parents nor our ancestors could ever have come into being.

To this group, we owe three things: life itself, the ways in which we may live that life, and the kin with whom we may associate to ensure its continuation.

Legitimate Preference can be defined as the disposition of mind that systematically and exclusively favors the group to which we owe these three things, rather than groups to whom we owe nothing.

I hope this disposition of mind can serve as an antidote to the morbid, stubborn tendency that has taken hold among Whites: a tendency ranging from suspicion to outright disgust at the idea of belonging to a genetic family.

At its extreme, this trend pushes our contemporaries to parade through the heavens of moral abstraction, forbidding their own kind from defending their genetic interests: to pass on, to protect, to prosper. As though being born White were a debt to be repaid as quickly as possible by dissolving into racial indistinction.

To all who still fight for this death-morality, Legitimate Preference brings bad news: we will repay nothing, and we will claim everything that is ours.

Exalting everything that is not ourselves should remain the eccentricity of a few marginal individuals, or a passing teenage fad, a cautionary example of what not to do. Yet the prolonged adolescence of our era has made this alter-worship permanent. Like a bad joke that drags on endlessly, at our absolute expense.

Whites, persuaded they are improving the world's "atmosphere," fall into racial renunciation the way others swoon. Fifty years into this anti-racist theater, men and women still suffer the fainting spells of their own "anti-racist vapors."

Against this, Legitimate Preference will act like a pungent smelling salt: repelling the sleepers, reviving the awakened. Those who believe morality should serve our genetic interests will see the obvious. The anti-racists will swoon. And nothing will change.

The premise of Legitimate Preference can be stated simply:

There is no such thing on earth as a generic *homo sapiens*. We are all varieties of *homo sapiens*, subspecies, if you like. Scientifically correct terminology calls these "ancestral groups." In everyday parlance: races.

This is not speculation. It is the basic reality of genetic groups, a reality some deny only to reassure themselves. For centuries, favoring one's own genetic and cultural group required no special permission. It was instinct.

What makes the articulation of Legitimate Preference necessary today is the cost, borne by Whites, of living in multiracial Western societies.

The cost is loss of ancestral lands, the destruction of quality of life, the endangerment of identity, safety, and prosperity.

If you think the generalization of Legitimate Preference would imperil universalist egalitarianism, let me confirm immediately: that is exactly the point.

Yet this concept should not be wielded with the frivolity of those who shock for shock's sake and are satisfied with that.

The first aim of the Preferist approach is to move beyond the very concept of "racism."

A concept may shock if it credibly promises improvement, if it carries with it a vision of what it claims to offer. That is the aim of the chapters that follow.

Legitimate Preference is not only a practical response to rising anti-White and anti-Western hatred; it is also a conception of the common good that draws lessons from the failure of multiracial societies. In this arena, the conventional solutions of the last 40 years have failed. Political activism, though necessary, has not stemmed the invasion of Western Europe.

So is there another way to restore territorial rights to Europeans?

If the idea of a White cultural and genetic nation has been exiled from the West, why not make it come to life again where no elite, or complicit populace, can reach it?

In the hearts of Europeans themselves, the first and last stakeholders.

After all, what could be more legitimate than what one feels for a lifetime? What could be more potent than a legitimate feeling suppressed by censorship for too long? What could be more resilient than a deep, rightful sentiment turned into a personal religion?

Before sparking visions of territorial reconquest, one must first form a community of mutual aid and dare to state publicly what is already in the heart.

Legitimate Preference is, first, legitimacy that dares to speak truth aloud, pooling resources to show the power of allegiance to this cause.

If we want collective strength, we must appear irrepressible.

The formula is always the same: discipline and joyful passion.

Religions, sects, and belief-movements all rest on this dual foundation: turning conviction into daily action, and attaching positive emotion to it.

If irrational doctrines can build large followings, why not a realistic one? Or will rationality itself be an obstacle?

Some chapters in this book deal with the need for strategic communication to counter that very risk.

Nietzsche noted that absurdity is not an argument against a thing's existence, but may even be a condition of its success.

I tend to agree. Moreover, being right often lulls us into believing in the supposed power of truth.

But truth by itself has no power. Truth is not a force. The rationality of our cause is unlikely to be enough on its own.

Legitimate Preference may only truly be born from the intensity of an emotion, from the sense of intolerable injustice or unforgivable waste.

It will be easier to prefer our own genetic community, every day and in every circumstance, as more of us come to find the opposite intolerable.

This book will not merely repeat what you already know. But the repetition of forbidden truths is itself a kind of book within the book. You may forgive, I hope, the déjà-vu.

I have also sought to present an identity concept without excessive intellectualism. In situations of legitimate defense (a cousin of Legitimate Preference), the rules must be simple. Endless analyses invoking arcane theories and historical anecdotes have never seemed effective.

Ordinary people fear breaking the law with what they feel in their hearts. The prospect of social ostracism terrifies them.

But if a law permitted people to punch you in the face, would you respect it? No. Well, no law forbids you to prefer your own. So you can put this book down and start now.

But if you have time, there is more.

Our digital media will not testify to what our era inflicts upon us. They are designed to consume our most precious resource, time, and to rewrite reality, erasing whatever challenges the mass mind.

Leaving a written trace is more necessary than it seems.

Many Whites now see that, in every land they built, false "minorities" have settled in and grown dominant, especially in prisons. Whites, the real minorities, are labeled the "majority," a lie that blocks any clear view of the demographic crisis.

Scientific correctness assists this denial, declaring race a "fiction." Which it is not.

Crimes against Whites are spun as "legitimate anger," or explained away sociologically, when they are not simply ignored.

Dissidents of both Right and Left, starved for an audience, claim the media are stirring us toward "civil war." According to them, the trap is division.

As though it would be paradise if only the media stopped occasionally praising "diversity."

Yet, in prisons, schools, villages, and cities, all indicators tell a different story: the media do not foment division, they silence anything that might cause it.

Every day, hundreds of thousands of Whites in France visit websites that break this silence. They do so to confirm they are not dreaming. A strange nightmare: certainty that we are awake.

But what then? Do we merely feed on anguish itself?

The official narrative insists that everything is "not too bad."

If you survive an Islamist attack in France and need counseling, you may well be assigned... a Muslim psychologist. He will "listen," but in truth he will be verifying your adherence to the dogma of *vivre-ensemble*.

This really did happen after the Bataclan massacre.

But, the "experts" assure us, hatred is White, anger is "diverse."

Hatred: a vile moral ugliness. Anger: a legitimate revolt. Two words that smuggle in an entire ready-made analysis.

Meanwhile, ad campaigns relentlessly pair White women with African men, and only White women are pressed to doubt motherhood. White virility is demonized as extremism, non-White virility exalted.

An entire mental atmosphere is combined with anti-White resentment, building an irreversible slope. The voluntary endangerment of our biological group is the deep anthropological trend of the 21st century.

Most intellectuals refuse even to look. Some marginal books touch the subject, but a leaden lid stays clamped on it.

Analysts dissect capitalism, liberalism, sovereignty. They explain immigration as a consequence of those systems. Their observations may be useful, but they do not yield a practical, daily strategy to improve our fate.

Cultural and national identities are defended endlessly, but the deeper problem is elsewhere.

National identity is the varnish. Biological identity is the wood. To understand strength, or collapse, look to the wood.

When a White is raped by a Black in prison out of racial hatred — a common reality, as Human Rights Watch admits — his national identity doesn't even exist.

These rapes, shrouded in silence across the West, reveal the volcano beneath our society. Terrified, we refuse to face what it means.

Western elites have not revolted against "global governance." They have revolted against their own peoples.

They have simply elected another people. That is the opposite of Legitimate Preference.

And the "majority" goes along.

Interior ministers fumble with broken buttons like malfunctioning machines.

The less sociology explains reality, the more socialist priests offer it sacrifices.

Do I need to spell out who is sacrificed?

Our situation is no longer merely political. It is communal, racial, chemical. We face not opponents but an atmosphere, worldwide and anti-White.

If we do not globalize White solidarity in return, we are already defeated.

The resentment of the weak against the strong, amplified by the internet, will not be calmed by rationality or commerce.

Among those people, some only voice it. Others act.

For now, the talkers are many. The doers are few. But the minority that prescribes action never sleeps.

Indoctrinated White sociologists are already pumping out fraudulent studies. In 2019, they "proved" the most common name among third-generation Maghrebis in France was... Nicolas.

It was not true. In fact, there were eleven.

Lying is the first verb of the ideology of mixing.

This hysteria and fraud reveal a short-lived ideology.

Speaking the highest truth we can, racial realism, may be the surest way to destroy it.

Legitimate Preference must also be the antidote to our deviant altruism.

The first common good is to prevent compassion from being hijacked.

White kindness must not be eradicated. It must be contained, framed, and re-educated.

Legitimate Preference is the frame in which it can operate without pathology.

If genes shape opinion, can there be a "recipe" to repair White altruism?

A new ideology, a new generation, a new social form?

This book will propose answers.

The first is this: act as the cells of an organism.

In biology, there is "self" and "non-self."

Your cells never work for another body. They prefer you. (Even if you are on the Left.)

Against all moral and egalitarian protests, the same rule holds for human genetic-cultural groups.

Our ancestors and descendants form our racial vessel. Treat it as a temporal organism. In preferring it, you act as your cells act toward you.

As said earlier, "*homo sapiens*" in the abstract does not exist. We all belong to subcategories.

Forensic labs prove this daily with DNA: ancestral groups.

Organ transplants prove it through incompatibilities. Diseases prove it through ethnic specificity.

Our way of belonging to *homo sapiens* is fundamental to who we are.

Different races may simply be a process of speciation underway.

This obliges us to think in the very long term.

But even now, one remark:

A universalist Leftist is someone who hopes his own cells will never follow his ideology.

And someone who opposes, on whimsical intellectual grounds, the natural diversification of life. Mixing is impoverishment.

French Theory philosophers, Deleuze among them, valorized this ideology with notions like "the body without organs," declaring the body's organic system a prelude to fascism.

Preferism, modeled on the body itself, was therefore already the enemy to be destroyed.

Placing moral awareness above biological continuity is an abuse of intelligence.

Individual consciousness allows escape from group determinism. That gap, well managed, enables art, philosophy, necessary solitude.

But, when exacerbated, it tears intelligence away from the genetic group from which it flows.

Legitimate Preference restores balance.

Our individuality spans the short term. Our genetic group spans the long.

Every individual is born in debt to it.

Legitimate Preference is the joyful currency with which we repay that debt.

Unlike financial or religious debts (such as original sin), this legitimate debt is joyful, because in repaying it, we strengthen both ourselves and our people.

Legitimate Preference makes us aware that we are more than individuals: we are a lineage across time, conquering space.

It deserves the advantage we can give it.

Once Upon a Time

I CAN ADMIT it now: I first understood what Legitimate Preference was by doing the exact opposite.

I was 13, fascinated by Aikido. The idea that one could subdue any opponent with a few subtle moves from this Eastern philosophy had conquered my mind. If someone offered you the chance to dissolve all adversity through a simple change of mindset and a few "magical" gestures, would you refuse? It was too beautiful to be false.

My grandparents had never had the chance to learn anything like that. Their lives were an endless mountain of labor. They saw the ocean for the first time at age 70. They lived in a small house at the end of an alley off Avenue de Paris in Rovalane (city name altered), which I visited almost daily.

Reaching that house was, for them, the culmination of indescribable effort that had begun in childhood. I know no one today who could manage it.

One day, at the entrance to that alley, an unbearable family moved in. Like a boil on a lip, they took root there and stole the one thing my grandparents cherished most: their daily peace.

Why? Simply because it was their nature. Dirty, vulgar, mocking, aggressive. They quickly drove out the other neighbors. If you were wondering, they were not poorer than us.

From time to time, they insulted my grandparents for no discernible reason, and let their children behave the same way. The father looked like a sedentary Gypsy, the others like nothing at all. Occasionally, they tried to "play nice," offering a forced "Good morning, Madame, good morning, Mr. T," accompanied by a smirk that even I, at 13, saw through. Then they went back to their trade in nuisance.

Entering or leaving that alley, coming home from the market or a walk, became a chore for my grandparents. The modest happiness they had finally attained in their brief retirement lost its taste.

The little pack did nothing strictly criminal. But this was still a time when simple incivilities were considered serious — at least outside the big cities. And my grandparents, who could not conceive of inconveniencing anyone, were unprepared for such behavior.

I was 13, and I loved my grandparents. But I did not prefer them.

Because I had decided not to believe in adversity anymore. "In Aikido, we have no enemy," the master had said. And life was the field where I applied this fascinating theory.

I knew I was disappointing them when I went to talk with the neighbors' kids, those boils, whose forbidden games drew me in. Even though I did not imitate them, and deep down I disliked what they did, I still went. Despite my family's reproaches.

I sincerely believed I had "risen above what my grandparents could understand." That was the Aikido theory. I had "canceled" the enemy in my mind, transcended the very concept. And I imagined reality would follow, since that is what the teaching promised.

Ideas tend to be stronger than reality in the mind of a believer.

"When thought is right, facts don't matter."

You cannot imagine how many Whites subscribe to this spiritual coaching maxim.

My grandparents eventually got used to it. The harassment continued. My grandfather passed away. And what I had degraded… remained. I had cut myself off from my ancestors in the name of an idea. And that, on a larger scale, is exactly what modernity invites us all to do.

You see the point, I suppose: my grandparents stand for our lineage, and Aikido represents the philosophy of our age (as for the boil-neighbors, I leave that to your imagination). One is seductive, the other austere. One promises to solve old problems effortlessly, the other promises nothing but effort. One wants to neutralize the other. And that other... is your lineage.

Yet, one is myth, the other real. We owe everything to our lineage, and nothing to the ideology in vogue.

The notion that we belong to a line stretching through time is rarely emphasized. And when it is, it sounds austere. But in truth, it is joyful and inspiring. I wish I had discovered it sooner.

It would take me five more years to finally escape that crippling hypnosis, when I met another kind of master.

Until then, I practiced pathological altruism, mistaking denial for a solution. Denial that adversity exists in reality, not just in the mind.

"Anti-racism is not an opinion. It is denial," as Father Mackenzie says.

That fundamental error is everywhere around us. The New Age that fits our era so well and seeps into every sphere of society is nothing but this error—the idea that if perception changes, reality will follow.

Even our classical philosophy had paved the way. Immanuel Kant claimed causality resides in the mind, not in nature. If that were true, time travel would be theoretically possible.

Ninety-one years later, Boltzmann proved him wrong, confirming what experience shows: causality is indeed external to us. Which means time is no illusion. Irreversibility is real. Unfortunately for me, and for my childhood errors.

Whites are dangerously vulnerable to ideas that claim to dissolve reality's difficulties. Of all these, the notion of the enemy is perhaps the one we most desperately want to banish with words. The moment a guru claims he can free us from all competition, all enmity with the great Other, we feel a childlike fascination. But gurus rarely test the theories they sell us.

To have a family is almost always to share the same enemies (which is not the same as sharing the same quarrels). The enemy is what reveals whether we are alone or not in adversity. And the enemy is not a concept — it is a fact of reality. The worst mistake is not even to deny this, but to lament it. One must accept it joyfully. The enemy exists. And when he comes, it is time to be family.

Every conflict tests group cohesion and demands that we give preference to our own. If you identify only as an individual, loyal to no group, then money will be your only shield against reality.

Strong communities, which never negotiate their solidarity, eventually gain both strength and wealth. So, choose your philosophy wisely for facing this time. Because, like our choices, it is irreversible.

The Big Brother

A FEW YEARS later came my reunion with my "big brother" in Preferism: Carl A.

Like me, he had been born into a family of Jehovah's Witnesses. The difference was that in my case, only one of my parents belonged. That single foot outside the movement was enough to save me from the dogma.

I think back to those endless meetings, where boredom reached such vertiginous heights that words themselves lose the power to describe them. Watching an ice cube melt would have fascinated me — if I had been allowed such a distraction during service.

A religion is just a sect that has made it big, and its success is measured by its penetration into art and culture. By that measure, you can see how utterly this sect failed.

I was eight when Carl slammed the back door of the Kingdom Hall in Rovalane (a town where, counterintuitively, Jehovah was installing more and more Muslims). It was minutes before the big Witness "mass," the moment when babies cry and children dream of being anywhere else.

Suddenly shattering the hushed atmosphere, Carl burst out for no obvious reason: "Go fuck yourselves with your bullshit!" And the door went *BAM* behind him, confirming the point.

Dissent from the dogma was usually timid in that rigid world. But this time, the congregation witnessed something more tangible than Jehovah himself: a boy, who would become my big brother, displaying intellectual autonomy that most of the room sorely lacked.

The background music resumed, the chabada-bada of biblical chant rolled on, and everyone returned to submission. Everyone, except a little boy of seven, who stood gaping — intimidated, intrigued, amused.

That boy was me. And I had just witnessed something else: the energy of a single person overturning the stupid gravity of a crowd drunk on obedience.

Ten years later, I turned 18. And I found Carl again, now a man, in a different setting — no ties, no Watchtower attire.

The laughter we shared by the main pool of Rovalane was not just joy that still sparkles in memory. It was instruction. For Carl taught through laughter.

Those lessons, absorbed in the chlorine spray of August 1991, still return with precision. They remind me of what my naïveté could have cost me in contact with "diversity."

By laughter, he gave me the first lesson you must give your children:

Show them how to strip away the fear that most of our people feel when confronted by groups of non-Europeans who delight in making us their prey.

How? By not respecting them at all. (I mean inwardly, as an attitude.)

That missing ingredient — total absence of intellectual respect for the colonizer — is precisely what today's French right-winger lacks. They cannot even make room for the thought. That was Carl's specialty.

It was the ground of my education. It is why I became a Frenchman of internal exile, one who cannot even fathom another mindset.

Carl never made jokes at the expense of our own, toward whom he was impeccably considerate. His ridicule was reserved solely for the hordes who overran the lawns and pools from 11 a.m. to 7 p.m., while the director let them do whatever amused them.

And you can imagine what "amused" them.

With precise, elegant cruelty, he sketched their moral ugliness and exposed their individual fragility. Carl had no fear of them at all. Unlike so many today, who don't even realize it, he felt no trace of fear before the rabble. His merciless, laughing gaze fascinated me.

By reserving his comic cruelty only for the enemy, while showing care and compassion to our own, he gave me an unmatched example. Even when dealing with me — naïve enough that he could have mocked me easily — he was patient. His careful pedagogy still remains etched in memory.

And then there were his lightning jokes, tossed off as naturally as breathing.

"Hey kid, hey kid!," he called to a fat Maghrebi teenager chasing a White boy across the slick tiles. Pointing to the floor as if to help, he said: "You dropped a kilo while running, look, right behind you."

The boy slowed his heavy steps to avoid slipping, his squat face contorting in incomprehension. For a passing instant, his look was almost touching. Then, vaguely realizing he was the butt of the joke for once, he scowled and turned back.

But preying only on the weak gives you a warped sense of intimidation. And that "asset for France" was about to learn it.

Carl's expression shifted. He moved in, grabbed the boy's neck, and pressed his forehead against his. I couldn't hear the low words, nor see his face fully, but the boy felt it: the temperature dropped ten degrees.

Carl's eyes told him clearly: this White was not like the others.

Carl's line of work involved jumping out of planes with heavy packs, the kind of work you don't brag about later. The kind where you sometimes keep tools close, even at the pool. Was that the case that day? I'll keep that to myself.

It could have ended badly for the cetacean. Not a lifeguard, not a pudgy director, not even a mob of vengeful thugs could have managed it — because Carl was not alone.

And as for "Majid," the whale-calf, he was the "leader" of the pack. If any reader feels tempted to sympathize, know this: Majid sometimes leapt onto the backs, literally the spines, of swimmers doing laps.

How many kilos can land on your body in a second when you're glide peacefully through your lane? You end up in the first-aid room with sharp pain, while his friends laugh: "Come on, it's just a joke!" And yes, they laughed plenty.

No measures were taken. You were left alone in humiliation. The staff only spoke of your condition, "maybe it's not too serious," never of the cause. The fat kid who crushed your spine wasn't the issue. Heaven forbid he rile his pals into doing worse.

"Don't worry, Madame. Do you want us to walk you out?"

No, idiot! I want you to rediscover some courage. I want you to stop talking as if these aren't enemies, and at least kick them out of the pool that *my* taxes funded.

Rovalane, its pool. France, its illegitimate preferences. And in between, a country sinking.

Thanks to that big brother, my laughter already contained the first building block of Preferism:

Never cultivate fear or respect for a group hostile to your own.

Fear conditions its bearer until he respects those he fears.

One day Carl engraved a phrase into my mind that has shaped my vision ever since. Between two jokes that had me doubled over, he said calmly and distinctly:

"Everything you see me do, you'll do too. But never respect anyone who tries to intimidate you. See them as they are. Never as they present themselves. They need your fear. Without it, they feel dominated. Do you understand?"

YES.

"Never respect those who seek to intimidate you." YES.

He knew words alone would have been mere rhetoric if he had not also preached by example. And I don't mean acting illegally, I mean an attitude. That is why nothing has overwritten it since.

Each word engraved itself in a separate kind of memory.

My grandparents thought you rarely get a second chance at a missed lesson. Yet mine was corrected at the pool, while watching whales run.

The Right to Prefer

MODERN WESTERN societies have taught us that preferring our own is a grave moral fault, a backwardness belonging to centuries past. This mistake has led straight to the daily tragedies of multiracial, crime-producing societies.

In religious communities, people renounce the right to prefer by consent — anyone is a brother simply by subscribing to a shared belief. In civil society, we renounce it without noticing, as anyone becomes our dear fellow citizen by simply holding a membership card. Our nations have become clubs.

"Good evening, sir, can you sing the *Marseillaise*? Oh, pardon me, your lady has just given birth? In that case, do accept our apologies, here is your card, please come in, your fellow citizens will serve the starters, have a splendid evening, sir."

If we pull ourselves together and think for a moment, this renunciation is neither useful nor pleasant. It strips us of what is ours without compensation, it keeps none of its promises, and it is not even desired by those who defend it. Even the anti-racists preach it, then carefully avoid practicing it.

Why continue the experiment? Why not reclaim our right to Preference, fully and openly, declared and assumed?

Prefer our own in hiring, in renting property, in access to services, in one's restaurant, exactly as we already do in love and in everyday relationships.

Can anyone order us to equalize our affections, to love our parents and strangers with the same intensity? Which of you is ready to give up privileging your children?

What legitimacy does the state have when it urges us to detach emotionally from our genetic-cultural family?

Shouldn't all those Western campaigns pushing the White-woman, Black-man pairing be treated as outright aggressions, political acts of contempt toward us? If a marketing campaign of that kind took place in, say, the Congo, the billboards would be ripped down in short order, and there would be an international media outcry against a racist, colonial attempt to subvert minds.

In truth, if we look at deeds rather than declarations, what do we find? We unconsciously favor our descendants by privileging our children, which is the most basic form of Legitimate Preference. But this attitude seems not to transfer to our contemporaries. A taboo falls on us as soon as Preference leaves the sphere of direct descendants. We are ordered to stop at narrow brotherhood.

To this, several thousand Whites in the West have already answered "NO," and have formed mutual-aid communities. *Les Braves* in France is the model case, a group that has spread across Europe and beyond, coordinating local community initiatives and bringing them together.

Their project is to sidestep rather than posture in futile activism, to stay out of the crosshairs of regimes that demean White natives, and to shield their children from cultural degradation and economic sidelining. This shield strategy preserves the essential inheritance passed down to us, our genetic-cultural legacy.

After all, we are the reason our ancestors labored so hard just a few decades ago. They consoled themselves with the thought that they were preparing us for an easier life. That effort was vertical Legitimate Preference, aimed at Whites not yet born. No justification was required then, none is required now.

Of course we have all heard the accusation that our Preference is simply the reflex of the privileged, gazing at the Third World sinking after we "pillaged" its "riches." I could not care less.

Try adopting that frame of mind. This, too, is Legitimate Preference, an economy of explanations no one will listen to anyway.

Is our essence's survival at stake, or the opinion of hypocrites who despise us?

Remember that *living together* is the only religion whose believers force non-believers to practice it in their stead.

A non-European may complain of being systematically rejected wherever he applies, of being passed over by a landlord, in short, of not being wanted. Because in truth, all of this turns on one thing: desire.

But no legislation has any business meddling with our lack of desire for them. The elites chose another people instead of us? Very well. Let them make room. We reserve ours for our children.

Can this fluid character of Legitimate Preference suffice to sabotage the regimes of constraint we live under? Can we derail the machine that plans to replace us, or at least refuses to oppose our replacement, simply by playing the Preference card?

In any case, Preference expressed by Whites for their genetic kin frightens Western states. It is the hard core of what they have fought ever since Western leaders "elected" another people. And it is, in fact, the only attitude that truly frightens Leviathan.

It is perfectly clear that we can no longer wait on the famous "National Preference," which depended on the equally famous "French awakening." The problem is that Westerners, the French foremost among them, are not asleep at all, they simply no longer care about their own. It is this lethargy that must be targeted and shaken by reopening the moral right to prefer oneself.

Legitimate Preference is also Legitimate Impatience, a stance that does not wait for government permission to be put into practice.

If examples speak to you more than principles, here is a story that illustrates the idea:

A bar manager in the center of my hometown once had a pricing policy that amused me so much it helped inspire Legitimate Preference. His menu listed only *cafés gourmands* — coffee served with small pastries — now about eight or nine euros in France. For a simple coffee, of course, that price would have been absurd.

When a European couple sat on the terrace and asked for coffee, he served it at about €1.50. When a young Maghrebi in a tracksuit, cap, and Nike shoes did the same, he brought a tray with the *café gourmand* and pastries and politely asked for nine euros. When the young man refused, the manager apologized and explained that at that hour the house served only *cafés gourmands*, not simple coffee.

Every downtown café complained that their usual European clientele fled at the hours when the thugs arrived to nurse a coffee for hours and disturb the peace. All of them, except him. He contented himself with weathering a few rumors of "racism."

For many people who have never reflected on the legitimacy of Preference, this anecdote is invariably shocking, because it highlights differential treatment that offends our egalitarian reflex. But the thought experiment invited by the pages that follow will show you that the opposite is what should now shock us all.

Remember, the politics of a country are like a river springing from a glacier. The glacier creates the river, not the reverse. Culture and the mental atmosphere become political direction, not the reverse. Nothing culture forbids becomes politically possible. Nothing culture and the mental atmosphere impose can remain informal for long. In time, the mental atmosphere hardens into law. And it is the margins that move societies with this strategy. We can use the same strategy.

Hence the importance of convictions that take root in our minds. Hence the importance of stating clearly your Preference for Whites, because it is this way of speaking that makes Preference go viral as an attitude.

What methods will make the Preferist stance viral? Keep in mind that Legitimate Preference has a single vocation, to impose itself gradually in people's minds as self-evident. It must become a shared culture, an idea felt as normal by everyone.

We must adopt, and make others adopt, two positions:

1. Modern states must evolve and become rational on this crucial point: native Europeans must fully exercise their imprescriptible right to Legitimate Preference.

2. Any state that claims the contrary must be constantly accused of backsliding into religious totalitarianism.

Before the complex societies of the West change their laws dramatically, we must first plant the ideological trees under whose shade our descendants will grow.

Preferring our own is a right we will recover through the practical philosophy set out in this book.

The Cost of
Hypocritical Preference

A BALANCED FAMILY that favors its own members sees the passage of time as an ally and a multiplier, because it makes its members grow and prosper. The same is true for any society that practices Legitimate Preference. Time then becomes the fertile soil for its genetic sowing and its technological victories, it even becomes the guarantor of progress, instead of being the destroyer of its achievements and its historical substance.

The first advantage of Legitimate Preference is not to save hundreds of billions in so-called humanitarian aid — money that has never produced the slightest positive effect on its supposed beneficiaries in the Third World. Humanitarian aid has no effect on those it claims to help, but it has a great effect on those who need relief from a guilty conscience. The main advantage is not the redirection of this public money into research, medicine, or assistance to the truly needy. Nor is it about building better political or economic partnerships than the ones we currently maintain with the South. Nor even the ability to face non-White ultra-violence with something other than flowers and candles.

The first advantage of Legitimate Preference may seem small, yet it is considerable: it restores the mental health of Western societies by eliminating what is draining their social capital: Hypocritical Preference. Instead of presenting the double game of the bourgeois Left, who spare themselves diversity while prescribing it to others, as a moral issue, it is more effective to present it as a social cost. In the eyes of the masses, what touches the economy carries more authority than moral arguments, which sound too much like mere opinions. And opinions are produced for free by everyone, so naturally no one wants those of others.

It is also something one can experience daily: living in a society where people despise each other ideologically and cannot understand each other without caricature is morally and psychologically costly, and it inevitably translates into economic cost. Almost all Whites are considered racist by the anti-White bloc. The non-racist Whites produce endless discourse that commits them to nothing, condemning them to a perpetual yet futile demonstration of non-racism. Hypocritical Preference always begins with an exhibition of diversity rhetoric, but the school-district dodges and the residential choices materialize what liberal Leftists truly have in their hearts.

It is often said that there is little difference between the life choices of a Ku Klux Klan member and those of a Socialist leader. From this perspective, the schizophrenic state of White public opinion in the West is alarming. Denunciations to employers, calumnies on social networks, constant insults and threats, all replace what people would truly inflict on one another if laws were suspended for only a moment. This literally erases public debate and turns every public statement into a trial. Which sociologist has ever quantified the democratic cost of this situation? Can a functional nation exist with such low social capital?

It must be noted that the Left has progressively trapped itself in an obsessive anti-Rightist role, highly damaging to itself. Is this what made the situation possible? The Left no longer considers democracy as a neutral framework that allows ideological and political alternation, but as a pretext to delegitimize everything that is not itself. Everything is evaluated through adherence to the "democratic values of the Republic," which are in fact presented as the values of universalist Leftism. This perception is a political bias with no intellectual justification. No rigged scale should ever be allowed to run a complex system. Such dysfunction is obviously enormously costly to any society that depends on the exchange of arguments and informed choice, but studies raising concern about this are nowhere to be found.

Hypocritical Preference stands at the intersection of absolute taboo and undeniable fact. White liberals, trapped in denial like common alcoholics, construct safe spaces of homogeneity they barely notice but could never live without. The calm, the assurance of being able to walk anywhere, the ability to meet the gaze of a stranger without fearing absurd or violent reactions, the ability not to dread a group approaching, not having to flee a neighborhood after four in the afternoon, the ability to lend a cigarette without it being a prelude to a knife attack, all of this and much more has been lost in most French cities. The privileged do not even need to admit it consciously, they feel it, and that is enough.

"Of course, I am not racist, you know me Patrick, but I had to get around the school district map, because Maxence and Bérénice are... very impressionable."

Politicians never admit that the ability to enjoy social homogeneity is now reserved for affluent Whites. But everyone knows that Hypocritical Preference often corresponds to a real estate market beyond the reach of modest Whites, even as the privileged still benefit from their abstraction of anti-racism. Professors, celebrities, TV anchors, executives, entrepreneurs, all of them practice a form of expatriation into racially privileged neighborhoods. There is indeed such a thing as White privilege, but it is not a system that benefits all Whites, only a caste of racial bourgeois who live in discreet enclaves. The occasional ethnic touch in their daily lives does not change the deeper trend.

This "living among one's own" can even be practiced on the edge of a racially replaced neighborhood, because territorial lines are drawn with precision. One street away, everything changes. A building in the middle of a replaced *département* can still be a White island in a Third World sea. Each supposed exception must be examined closely, because the Whites of Hypocritical Preference love to signal that they live in "diverse neighborhoods."

There are also less affluent Whites who choose Shameful Preference, paying for it with geographic isolation. These other refugees pass under the media radar. Not understanding what they are truly fleeing, they even pass under the radar of their own awareness. In the isolated village of Saint-Nicolas-des-Biefs in central France, a few hundred Whites represent this reality found everywhere in the country. They enjoy, without quite understanding why, a "privileged" environment, but at the price of living far from everything. A strange White privilege that must exile itself in a digital and economic desert just to endure a little longer.

When you talk with these inhabitants, you hear scattered traces of mild anti-racism, typical of city centers, as well as a near-hostile suspicion toward anyone who speaks too openly of the harassment Whites face. This is explained by the phenomenon of White flight that has filled these villages with new rural migrants from replaced cities: they need to not draw too much attention to their strange privilege.

One anecdote illustrates the hidden costs of Shameful Preference. A newcomer found himself in charge of the summer pig roast in the village restaurant. His half-dreadlocked blond hair revealed his politics, and his bulky lumberjack look fit the "local color" new rural migrants sometimes cultivate. The restaurant was run by former Parisians who came to "recharge" far away from everything. This emblematic dish implies not only a non-Muslim clientele, but above all the absence of a significant Muslim population nearby. What percentage of Marine Le Pen sympathizers would one find among the guests?

A group of 50 tourists, escaping the diversity of the cities for a few days, signed up for one of these pig roasts. But during the meal, conversations became too explicit. The man turning the spit listened with growing indignation. He said nothing at the time, but once the tourists had left, he demanded explanations and angrily told them never to return to the village. Of course, no one took him seriously.

People who isolate themselves geographically and accept meager lives refuse others the same tranquility, simply because those others embrace consciously what they themselves practice shamefully. How long must this persist before it is recognized as a troubling dysfunction? Why is there no sociology mapping White flight? Must sociology remain hostage to political activists?

At first glance, the Whites of Shameful Preference avoid this reality because it would generate unbearable cognitive dissonance and social costs in their own lives: loss of friends, networks, income. Yet the hidden cost may be even greater. All these hatreds, this ideological schizophrenia, can it really be cured with more indoctrination?

The same mindset appears elsewhere. When Clément Méric, a well-born bourgeois White, leaves his enclave to attack Esteban Morillo for buying Fred Perry clothes, it is Hypocritical Preference in its high-bourgeois form, energized by youth. "You cannot have access to White homogeneity. You do not have the right to prefer living among your own," is what his unconscious would have said. Yet, he reserved that very same privilege for himself.

This mindset may enrich psychoanalysts, but it ruins civil peace and poisons politics. It pits users of the same services and inhabitants of the same country against one another, people who nonetheless need access to tranquility and the ability to exchange with different opinions. That is the very condition of intellectual maturity.

In a caste society like France, which knows nothing of equality or liberty for those who inhabit it, Hypocritical Preference acquires explosive power. It turns White enclaves into lucrative markets, accessible only to senior executives and system insiders who preach tolerance in public and buy their way out of it off-camera.

The first advantage of Legitimate Preference is therefore to liberate the emotional life of citizens, since preference is an affection, and to bring about a massive return to reality. Without this, hatred and absurdity will remain the normal modes of expression between the two clashing ideologies of the country.

Depriving citizens of the right to prefer whom they wish is in fact a religious intrusion into politics. Buddhism calls this non-preference *uppekka*, a rare mental state that permits higher meditations and entry into *Nibbana*, the end of rebirth. Is this also the project for the West?

This schizophrenia does not just consume logic, it generates distress and then resentment, which in turn feed the violent projects that the media delights in deploring. The country reached a level of alarm after the Bataclan massacre carried out by North African Muslims, but no mainstream media dared say so. A woman living ten meters from the concert hall entrance witnessed the massacre. She expressed her legitimate fear on Facebook, admitting that radical Islam terrified her. Her family and friends instantly condemned her and cut ties. This was someone who had literally seen war wounds and felt the breath of a dying man on her skin. Her family's compassion evaporated. That is what anti-racism does to its followers and to its victims.

A doctor monitoring her health even asked, "Have you managed to reconcile with Islam and Muslims, Madame?" Words of breathtaking stupidity. And in the psychological support cell for survivors, a veiled Muslim woman was assigned to guide the exchanges. Imagine Charles Manson running therapy for the families of his victims.

A fellow musician, learning of her new "Islamophobic" opinions, threatened to pass her name to radical Muslims in hopes they would act. This is the Leftist artist in all his splendor: too cowardly to strike directly, but eager to outsource violence to others. And we are supposed to build a common nation with this.

How can such a collection of irreconcilable enemies form a country? Why prolong the ideology that fuels this fire, at the cost of Western social capital?

The man I describe lived securely in a White Parisian neighborhood, or what remains of it, yet he acted as a potential aide-de-camp to Islamist terrorists. Thousands of Whites soaked in Hypocritical Preference share the same disposition, and nothing in Western culture makes them ashamed of it.

If his intentions had led to tragedy, how should the victim's husband or son have reacted? Why does society get so worked up about the vanishingly rare "far-right" attacks, while it does everything to produce them?

One of the hidden costs of this system is the emigration of White brains, who instinctively feel the country is hostile to them, that living there is punishment. This threatens not only France's own economic and technological development, but the peace of Europe, for halfway through the replacement process France will have become a Muslim country armed with nuclear weapons. What will its relations with its European neighbors be then?

This scenario may seem fantastical. But tomorrow it will not. Other scenarios once dismissed as "far-right nonsense" are now reality. The West of 2050 cannot exist without meeting the Preferist challenge. The social cost imposed by anti-racist dogma is absurd and unsustainable. The wall will fall.

For now, White preference is treated as the very essence of what politics exists to combat. Paradoxically, that may help us rediscover that the purpose of a nation is to preserve the continuity of genetic transmission, and that without it, the very reason we pay taxes evaporates.

No improvement is possible until the forbidden words are hammered daily in the public square: Legitimate Preference. Legitimate Preference protects against aversion and provides an escape from hatred. Hatred takes root only when people are forced to endure the unendurable, and it multiplies when one must play a permanent comedy with oneself and with others.

By offering only Hypocritical or Shameful Preference to Whites, Western societies condemn them to hatred while demanding that they banish it. No legislation can call itself modern without integrating the notion of genetic Legitimate Preference. All other options must be presented as civic regression and theft of rights.

Tactically, illegitimacy must become for the Right what inequality is for the Left. "What is the legitimacy of a Constitution that asks me to renounce Preference for my own?"

For too long we have avoided using the Left's tricks, in the name of our moral superiority. But they are not tricks, they are winning tactics in democracy. The raw material of democracy is emotion, not ideas. We must therefore use levers that reach emotions.

The struggle against illegitimacy and against the social cost of White liberal hypocrisy can become our favorite hammer. Political concepts are nails. And politics is done only with hammer blows.

The Redefinition of Words

THE REAL challenge for us is probably not to march onto the battlefield of logic to persuade the masses. People flee argumentative rhetoric because it always seems murky and uncertain. Trying to persuade them would be like emptying a lake with a spoon while it is raining. But there is a legal way to "cheat," to reach a favorable outcome faster: the redefinition of words and the privatization of concepts. To redefine a word is to give it a new meaning. To privatize a concept is to use an idea so that it serves only our interests. The notion of the "exploited" fulfills this function. If there are exploited, then there must be exploiters, and they must be stopped. In the phrase, "We demand equal airtime for the exploited, against bosses who enjoy permanent access to television," exploitation is presupposed, and the debate is reduced to speaking time. Every time you use the word "exploited," whatever you say with it, you are scoring points for the Left.

If you want to defend the idea that bullfighting must be abolished, never ask, "Should bullfighting be abolished?" Put on the table the metal instruments used to stab the bull. Then you are instantly 30 points ahead. Then use the notion of "de-tradition." "How should we de-tradition the relationship between man and animal?" The presupposition is smuggled in: it must be done, and your goal is reached before anyone is conscious enough to oppose it. That is the privatization of the concept, and it is a trick the Left uses constantly.

But a redefined word is even more insidious. It must give the impression of greater precision, of being more suited to the situation, and it must make the old definition look outdated. Once you attach this new dimension to a word, you alone control its meaning, you alone can speak about it with authority, and you can monopolize airtime indefinitely if your idea captures the spirit of the age.

This is the case with philosophical notions such as "minority." Gilles Deleuze redefined it as "dominated," "subject to the power of a dominant majority," for activist purposes. This deliberate shift in meaning, presented as "concept," prevents people from saying that most Third World populations, the so-called "minorities," have long since become majorities, thanks to the pathological altruism of "French doctors" that exploded their demographics. It is on this falsification of "minority" that the idea of "systemic racism" was grafted, making it even harder for the public to sort truth from lies.

Spreading what I call "verbal counterfeit" often allows one to exploit misunderstandings and the intellectual torpor of the masses. The philosophers of "French Theory" could indeed produce simple concepts when it was about arming street activists. They reserved the incomprehensible ones for intellectual posturing and semantic trickery. Because of "minorities," we are prevented from even thinking about our own reduction to minority status, and its consequences are never acknowledged publicly.

Here, the counter-attack could be simpler than against privatized concepts. Consider this short exchange between a high school history teacher and a Preferist friend in 2021: "You cannot call yourself a victim of racism because you are not part of an oppressed minority. Your minorities are actually majorities on this planet. You do not understand the meaning of the word. Minority does not mean fewer in number, it means dominated. Use only the word 'dominated' in that case. Otherwise you are lying twice, once about the explicit meaning and once about the specific meaning. But minority has already changed meaning, what you are doing is nothing more than reactionary misuse of an outdated sense."

Ideological autism pays.

In reality, Whites are both minorities and dominated. They are the only people on earth who cannot finish the sentence "I am proud to be…" with their own name. Exposing conceptual trickery can be rewarding, but it depends on context. What works at a café table does not work in a university lecture hall. No method is truly universal. Ideological battles are territorial, and this must be remembered before testing certain pointed questions:

What is the only people in the world who find it shameful to defend themselves?

What is the only people in the world who are told they have no ancestral homeland?

What is the only people in the world who must never worry about being made a minority?

These questions can crack universalist dogma, sometimes even shift middle-class White opinion. Interrogative rhetoric remains useful, but it requires a brave agent and a strong speaker. Privatized concepts, however, work on their own.

The word "racism" acquired this autonomy after being privatized by Third Worldist militants in the 1980s. For 30 years it lay in wait until it could assume its full meaning: "vigilance against White identity." One could reply that the word was always designed as an accusation against Whites, and that would be true. The semantic slide was predictable. But the important point is this: the anti-White bloc did not win this battle through debate. They won it by redefining concepts, by shifting meanings.

Today, "racism" has even lost its original meaning of "racial hatred." It would be extremely difficult to restore it. To roll it back would require compliant media, and we do not have them. What to do? Sometimes, when someone pulls hard enough to rip something from your hands, the smart move is to let go. "Only Whites can be racist? You are sure? Fine."

In that case, only the victims of this racism can describe what it feels like. That must be conceded. But in turn, only Whites know

precisely what their racism consists of. Since they are the only producers of it, they alone can define it. Let us admit publicly what it is
we are accused of. Because, like in Plato's cave, the "victims" of White
racism perceive only the shadow of what they speak about.

In reality, our "racism" consists in an absence of desire for other
peoples, an absence we do not dare express for fear of hurting them.
Everything here is about desire. We may sometimes be curious, but
it is never love for the other. Between their expectations and what we
offer, nothing coincides. This absence of desire explains why we constantly, often unconsciously, keep our distance from peoples whose
apparent desire is to live near us, and specifically among us. Their
narcissistic injuries come from the gap between their expectations
and what we have to give. The issue is not our psychic re-education, a
mad and illegitimate political project, but their immaturity.

The formula shifts from "You Whites must question yourselves"
to "Gentlemen non-Whites, grow up. We do not possess what you demand." Very few Whites can publicly accept being "racist," but many
could perhaps accept this paradigm: "The desire for living together
cannot be commanded."

Of course, the Third Worldist camp will endlessly play its guilt
card to stay on the terrain of emotional war: "You plunder Africa,
we are only taking reparation," and so on. This is yet another reason
never to argue, but to oppose a "conceptual wall." Only real dialogues
of the deaf end one day, every other exchange ends with the surrender of the more altruistic party.

Modern societies truly believe they can extort mandatory love
from us. Like old religions, they assume we owe an emotional tax.
"You shall love your illegal migrant as yourself." No. This childish
demand must be rejected with the argument of Preference.

Rather than debate at such a level of stupidity and hypocrisy, we
must put into circulation words with new meanings, words that form
a barrier. Consider this speech, once famous in France, by former
president Nicolas Sarkozy:

What is the objective? It will cause controversy, but the objective is to meet the challenge of miscegenation. The challenge of miscegenation is what the twenty-first century presents to us. France has always known this challenge, and in rising to it, France is faithful to its history. It is consanguinity that has always caused the collapse of civilizations. France has always been mixed. France has mixed cultures, ideas, histories. France, which has known how to mix its cultures and histories, has built and produced a universal discourse because it itself feels universal in the diversity of its origins. Ladies and gentlemen, this is the last chance. If this republican voluntarism does not work, then the Republic will have to adopt more coercive methods, but we have no choice, the diversity at the base of the country must be reflected in the diversity at its head. This is not a choice, it is an obligation. It is imperative. We cannot do otherwise. At the risk of considerable problems. We must change, and we will change.

NICOLAS SARKOZY, Palaiseau, December 17, 2008.

Was this some kind of delirium that seized the French president that day? Lost in his actor's role, he publicly demanded that the French submit to a program of generalized miscegenation. Was he even faintly aware that miscegenation implies a sexual act, which by definition requires consent? Prudently, the Élysée removed from the official transcript the words, "If this republican voluntarism does not work, then the Republic will have to adopt more coercive methods."

Whatever the case, he revealed the exact model behind every political project that imposes forced coexistence: rape.

This is why Legitimate Preference has a legal and political dimension. To prefer is not only to claim the right to give advantage to one's own, it is to discharge a duty toward them, and it is to want a certain type of society.

Whatever our level of awareness, we all have an interest in living in a society that does not criminalize the emotional life of its citizens, that frees them from the duty to love what they do not love. The result will be a society where White homogeneity is no longer dragged before the courts, but recognized legally as private right and philosophically as public good.

That is the discreet power of words reforged in meaning: their effects are visible only once the opposing camp has lost the battle and is left arguing in vain.

Good Slogans, Bad Slogans

A T A TIME when no one reads anymore, slogans have probably become more powerful than books. A slogan asks no permission before entering your head and forcing you to hear a truth. It respects no code of politeness, no culture, it addresses the brain directly. Some slogans are like little haiku of truth that slam into your mind: "Anti-racism is a code word for anti-White." Others only leave you puzzled, such as "Impossible is not French," and they paralyze action.

Slogans reveal a lot about an ideological camp, about what we understand, about our state of mind, about our ability to communicate, about our vision of society, about our morale, and above all about our nerve. The war of slogans is often underestimated in its positive or negative effects, and the principles that allow one to score points with them are often misunderstood.

Let me reflect on two slogans I have used myself, slogans that had some success but may have held back broader acceptance of our ideas: "It's OK to be White" and "White Lives Matter." These are two well-known formulas coined by the American alt-right and repeated worldwide by identitarian activists or simply by intellectually honest people. I like these two slogans for their irony and the way they expose mass hypocrisy. When I saw them spreading online, it seemed obvious to me that reaffirming these truths and letting common sense do the work was the right strategy, as if obviousness itself had power.

But here's the scoop: it has none.

At first, I thought these slogans would trap the anti-White camp and build consensus. That never happened. In the abstract, the two statements are indeed undeniable. Of course it is "OK" to be White, and of course our lives have the value of human lives. Yet both formulas were violently rejected by mainstream society. And when I say violently, I mean physical violence against Whites, sometimes fatal, during the Black Lives Matter movement. "Kill a White on sight," "White men, women and children, you are the enemy," and "Hate is OK if directed at WHITE FAMILIES" were among the slogans proposed by the sympathetic "Black Lives Matter" movement.

We discovered that it was possible to affirm publicly that it is not "OK" to be White, and that "White lives" do not really matter. So what went wrong? What these two slogans had in common is that they lent themselves to the counterattacks they suffered, simply because they beat around the bush. To beat around the bush is to not go directly to the core of your own message. It is to be afraid of what you have to say. By not saying things as they are, you conceal your true feeling, and you give your enemy the power to interpret your message. You allow him to divine your "real" intentions, and when an enemy uncovers your intentions, it is never to valorize them. It also shows him that you remain beneath the truth, that you are testing his intelligence. This is always taken as hypocrisy, weakness, or sly trickery. Frankness and precision are probably the only "extreme" positions that actually win in debate.

Almost no one supposes that "It's OK to be White" really means nothing more than that. Because the banality of the message suggests there must be more behind it. The slogan actually asks the reader to take a side. It asks him to validate a statement too naïve to be honest. In reality, it lures him into reacting to a White racial affirmation, and he feels trapped. He knows that it is not so "OK" to be White at the moment, just as he knows you are extracting his assent. The same goes for "White Lives Matter," which should bring agreement, but instead generates hostility and resentment. Claiming an egalitarian position in the middle of the furious magma of Black and leftist grievances could only backfire. Of course White lives matter in the abstract, but not in the context of Black Lives Matter. In that moment, the phrase could only be taken as diminishing the importance of Black lives, as a way of taunting a non-White crowd itching for a fight after the George Floyd affair.

Beating around the bush with ironic formulas allows your interlocutor to bet on your bad faith, which incites him to reject your message. Far from being useless, these two formulas are actually failures in terms of agit-prop. They increase our reliance on irony, already constant, without giving us any lever to advance our cause or to make our arguments go viral. Yes, they bring laughter to our side, but that laughter was already with us. Above all, by circling around the truth, these formulas miss the target and waste precious media time, because every formula leaves a trace in the public memory.

These slogans reflect a context. Whites are told to renounce their identity under pressure from groups that harass them. Massive anti-White orgies of punishment, as plaintive and grotesque as they are, ritually reverse the roles of victim and executioner. The media fabricate artificial legitimacy for any form of anti-White rage, because it feeds their pathological self-hatred. These same media constantly remind Whites of the sanctions they risk if they dare affirm their identity, while every other people is free to proclaim theirs on Western soil. It is enough to drive anyone mad.

It is normal that ironic pro-White formulas have appeared everywhere in reaction to this injustice. In fact, the civility of the White response astonishes intelligence services. But these slogans do not reflect a considered communication strategy. They are clever, biting, and sometimes witty, but they circle around the truth instead of stating what we really think and want. It is tempting to use irony and to mock our enemies, but irony does not serve us. At this stage, it is the enemy who mocks us, so irony only benefits him.

What if the effectiveness of a slogan, for us, lay simply in saying directly what we really think? In our condition of dispossession, we cannot demand less than the right to Prefer. A slogan that says simply, "I just prefer Whites, you cannot understand," would be shocking in a positive way, totally frank, and 100% innocent. Could anyone suspect a hidden agenda? No, because everything is admitted. Could anyone mount a learned analysis of the message? No, because nothing is hidden. Could anyone challenge it legally? No, it is legal to have a Preference. Could anyone shame it morally? No, a Preference cannot be commanded.

Since our society is a training camp for delegitimizing Whites' preference for their own, it requires effort to look our deep sentiment in the eyes. But there is strength in looking at what no one dares look at. There is even greater strength in daring to say it publicly, without irony. Faced with the permanent sarcasm of the Left, the truest tone may well be the honesty of authenticity. "Sorry, I prefer Whites" may be the most devastating way to ruin all the work of the anti-White camp. First, because it allows no intellectualization. In our situation, discussion must be prevented, a wall must be built. No discussion with the enemy has ever been truly won, no logic has ever advanced us an inch. Second, it is a way of saying, "All your efforts were in vain, we are more resistant than before." Demoralizing the enemy is important, especially when he is obsessed with controlling your thoughts and your emotions.

That a clear and concise slogan can replace a thousand debates is exactly where we stand today. Since debates no longer serve their purpose, and since intellectuals spend their lives telling Whites they are angry for the wrong reasons, isn't it better for a slogan to speak for us? For a radical identity slogan to work, it must be free of aversion and negativity. Only say what you can affirm publicly. That is probably the only path to shifting opinion. Do not even try to mock opponents, as that would still mean wanting discussion. Let me repeat: the goal of a true argument is to end discussion.

We must present what is in our hearts, say the truth without trickery, without sneering, without bluffing. People know that feelings cannot be changed, it is that feeling they must be made to feel. Our best arguments are affects presented with immovable audacity.

Legitimate Preference is ultimately a way of short-circuiting implicit messages and hints, a way of heading directly to the end of the exchange, without argument, rather than dancing around the subject. I stress this point because I believe we are also an army of slogan-soldiers, of words and debates. If speech had no effect, intelligence services would not bother attending conferences, cafés, union meetings, online forums. I believe we must become the masters of the intellectual atmosphere through mastery of slogans and formulas. That requires more discipline than creativity.

In France, the identitarian right often feels it must constantly invent new lines and strategies. I think the opposite. Our strength is discipline, our weakness is too much analysis and too many speeches. Repeating one and the same Preferist line, often without argument, is more important than producing a thousand demonstrations in the face of the deluge of anti-identity sophistry our opponents manufacture.

The consumer society is in fact a society of consumers who want to hide their responsibility and their power to choose. Let us make them consume Preference in every form, by spreading our slogans. Our war is where we still have room to maneuver: in communication.

Let me end this chapter with a model slogan:

"In reality, everyone prefers Whites. We are just the last ones to dare say it." Which can be shortened to: "In reality, everyone prefers Whites."

The point here is not absolute accuracy, but a slight exaggeration to force the mind to engage. Deep down, all people who do not particularly like Whites often still prefer them.

You go on holiday with people you love, and when you have the choice, you choose neighbors you prefer to be surrounded by. You try to get hired in companies Whites build, you entrust them with your luggage at the airport while you use the restroom, you are reassured when they run your child's school, when they run the nation's finances, when they handle fires, when they are the surgeon you see before your eyes close.

You may not like Whites, but you know your safety, your future, and your comfort depend on them. For all their imperfections, you know they do not cultivate indifference. On the contrary, they are the people of concern for others, the people of moral unease.

The Power of Demanding

Y OU WILL have noticed that the Left resorts to hysteria every time it is confronted with facts. Its method, playing the raging autistic the moment you mention the social performance of non-Europeans, is extraordinarily effective. Legitimate Preference needs its own method of communication and persuasion.

No one remembers the endless list of Maghrebi criminals that National Front MP Marie-France Stirbois read aloud at the National Assembly in the 1980s, a list of murders, rapes, rackets, and assaults committed in just six months by that prolific community. No one remembers it because Leftist hysteria worked. Hysteria is how the Left demands silence from the Right. Cold or hot, it demands intolerance in the name of Good.

That, precisely, is what we should want. Not hysteria itself, but the power it secures: the power to silence, to redefine what ideas have the right to exist, to make the opponent bend, to force him constantly into defense and justification. None of these tools are state instruments. They are all in our hands, especially the will to demand and to force our demands to be taken seriously, by harassing public opinion. Because public opinion can be reforged.

From this point of view, the conventional Right wastes precious time. It cloaks itself in righteousness, common sense, dignity, good manners. For too long it has retreated step by step in the shadow of "what will people say?," like an old spider destined to be crushed behind an antique piece of furniture. This obsolete armament must be discarded, a new language must be spoken. Why not steal from the enemy what works?

Observe one thing: the woke movement is only secondarily mad; above all else, it is in tune with its age, the age of demands. The demands of the woke are centered on the body, and that is a theme we must seize. But more important than the theme is the method. Can you imagine demanding Celtic, Slavic, and Germanic pride, celebrating European beauty? That will must be acquired. It can be trained. Shyness and embarrassment are dams, and they can burst.

We analyze woke ideology too much, criticizing it philosophically, and we forget that it secures obedience with a little makeup and a lot of tears. Why are we not obsessed with the methods of victory? That is all we should desire, instead of burning our energy in intellectualism. No analysis is as exhilarating as victory.

The moment a method works, especially an enemy method, we must find the principle, adapt it, and move to testing. Forget the emotional reactions the enemy provokes in us. Our emotions must be communication strategies, not raw affects. In a spectator society, ideas must become theater, emotions must be militant. Gustave Le Bon rightly argued that the crowd has a psychology totally distinct from its individual members. That psychology thinks only in terms of emotion. But emotion requires social proof to feel legitimate. And nothing is more powerful as social proof than a discourse that claims to be scientific. Once again, the Left shows us its tricks, and we should not ignore the lesson.

By using sociology as the systematic explanation of the disorders caused by Afro-Maghrebi communities in France, the Left made a tactically shrewd choice. This university discourse, born in the 1960s, endlessly repeats its pseudo-scientific dogma in the realm of violent crime. It insists that the link between low-IQ immigration and delinquency is fictitious. The main actors of this criminality never read sociological texts, yet they benefit enormously from this pseudo-science, which provides rational cover for their impunity. In reality, it is genetics that explains the structural tendencies of our societies as well as the DNA of the prison population.

Prisons filled with "fifty shades of immigrants" are explained away by sociological dogma that persuades the public to continue the migration experiment as if nothing were wrong. Did this sociological discourse, endlessly recycled by the media, help prevent a rightward electoral shift? This is a question worth asking. What matters most is the conclusion: any politics that intends to last must forge alliances with intellectual cover that pretends to explain daily reality.

A discourse that carries scientific authority and imposes itself in the public consciousness is the first scepter of influence. Without that permanent lie, the Left would have to confront the crowd with the complexity of reality. But the crowd has no interest in reality. Its brain can absorb only a well-told story, not a learned explanation. This is why it rarely retains our Right-wing explanations and rarely "rewards" us at the ballot box. We do not offer it grand, reassuring promises.

Notice also how France, obsessed with denying the existence of races, resists the woke only in its supposedly "racialist" claims, even though the woke also deny biological race. But the mere fact that they utter the word "race" and keep the concept alive is intolerable to regimes intent on erasing the reality. This means woke ideology is not opposed by the establishment because of its absurd demands, but only because of its racialist view of the world. The egalitarian universalist boomers are confronted with a new kind of anti-racism that displaces them and makes them look outdated. They reply on the plane of morality and culture, while ignoring the essential: demands.

The consequences of a successful scandal are always the same. Respectable society works tirelessly to avoid uproar and concedes almost everything, as long as the screamers go silent and the taboo words are no longer spoken. Whites resistant to all these demands, conservatives above all, generally retreat into commentary, into reflections on the "common good," into rationalizations and analyses.

They are so wise, prescribing virtue, reproving the blameworthy. They are as exciting as a prescription slip. They have made it their style and think it is a strength. It is not. Only rational fanaticism, fanaticism of thought, able to wield the full emotional spectrum of political marketing, can rival the Left and defeat it.

Let me venture an aside prompted by a remark a mother recently made to me. What about those who will not yet dare call themselves Preferists, but who still want to participate in the war of attrition against public opinion and state messaging? In other words, how can one advance Preferist demands without naming them?

At bottom, all that non-Preferist society offers us is the gradual escalation of threats linked to the permanence of multiracial societies. We are asked to raise our tolerance threshold step by step until permanent danger becomes normal. "Wrap your forearm around your neck in case of a throat attack. Better a slash on the arm than a severed jugular." That is the current trend. It will end with self-defense classes covered by social security.

This is what François Bousquet has called "the insurance society," where insurance companies are the last bulwark against chaos. A handful of decision-makers decide whether the level of insecurity the people endure is acceptable, all while as they themselves remain sheltered. And if disaster strikes, society offloads everything onto the insurers, who become the only interlocutors. Insurance as the last social bond before death. The only intolerable cost for such a society is native revenge. Just look at how the survivors of the Bataclan who refused reconciliation with their murderers' religion have been treated. Patrick Jardin, father of Nathalie, murdered at the Eagles of Death Metal concert, is constantly vilified by the media for his "hatred." *Libération* portrayed him as "a lost soul, muttering against Arabs, driving an oversized SUV, millionaire owner of France Cars," yet they carefully omitted the hatred he regularly receives from Leftist survivors who accost him for criticizing immigration policy.

Communities that group together to demand the defense of their interests become the only interlocutors in the insurance society, which no longer recognizes individuals. Only permanent harassment has proved effective in bending public power. The theme of security demands could justify a war of attrition the state cannot suppress. Becoming allergic to insecurity, the way Femen became allergic to patriarchy, may be the best entry point for those unwilling to assume Preferism openly out of fear of punishment for their opinions.

By habituating us to danger, the insurance society has blurred our vision. That danger is statistically identical to what Preferism fights. To see it clearly, take two weeks of holiday in Slovenia or Hungary. You will return with a list of threats you no longer wish to endure, and the link to Preferism will be obvious.

Life in multiracial society is an experiment without conclusion. We oscillate between denial, crimes, sociological explanations, and denial, crimes, sociological explanations. Even legitimate questions become suspect, and therefore forbidden. How long can you look a "diverse" group in the eyes before "some of them" decide to assault you for that alone? How many cigarettes must you carry to avoid a knife attack if you refuse one? Will social security reimburse them, given that refusing a cigarette has become more dangerous than smoking it?

When even basic questions cannot be asked, the time has come to demand what you no longer dare even to think. Demand safe spaces, White-only spaces, hotlines for teenagers attacked for being White, inquiry committees, Senate hearings, working groups. Is such a level of demand conceivable for most Whites who see the situation? For many, no. But the principle of demand works by emulation. The first to dare motivates others. The tenth is reassured. The hundredth assumes it has always been obvious.

Hurl accusations of endangerment, display our wounds, dramatize. Nowadays, it is impossible to exaggerate on these subjects, as you yourself have seen. We could constantly put our opponents on the defensive, force them to waste time and energy on rebuttals that we would sabotage with fresh accusations and even greater demands. More safe spaces, more security, more guarantees that it will never happen again. If any strategy has a chance to bear fruit, it is this one, because we have seen it work for the other side so often. Reverse the roles. Accuse permanently. Suffocate them. And never forget: the reasonable Right is never heard. Our society hears only screams, not wise voices.

Women can carry particular weight in this battle, since it requires an administrative front. "My children need a doctor who resembles them. My youngest was afraid of the one we saw last time." Say no more. The secretary will infer what she must. The first mother who sends such a message will need courage or naivety, better still. The tenth will no longer hesitate. The hundredth will assume it was obvious long ago. If the messages converge on the same target, even better. No individual can resist indefinitely the eruption of a sustained crowd movement. In our situation, to demand is to harass everything beneath the ministerial level.

Yes, many of us will hesitate and retreat. But we have gone from the trenches of Verdun to sending emails of complaint. As challenges go, do you think this is impossible when the alternative is civilizational death? Demanding the right to Prefer a European doctor is only a tiny beginning, albeit something that may seem unimaginable today, even more so than refusing to give up your seat on a bus. But why? If your preference for a White doctor shocks those around you, ask them this: what business is it of theirs? And why would it be an advantage to live in a society that makes such a right inadmissible? Yes, such a society would offend those it does not prefer, but that is true of every unrequited love. Should we legislate against unreciprocated affection?

Whatever your arguments, when you press your demands, never compare your claims to those of non-White communities. That would start an unwinnable debate, because their concepts are designed to score points only within their own camp. What must be built is a specifically European demand, not an abstract exercise in philosophy. Above all, you are not seeking debate, you are seeking results. Who would prefer the delivery to the baby? No one demands a discussion. We demand an outcome.

One last point: formulated with enough boldness, a shocking demand can intimidate. A demand is often rejected only because it stands alone, because no one else pitches in their voice. Not because it is illogical. If coherence were an effective weapon, we would have won long ago. The success of a demand depends more on the flow of words of the one making it than on its substance. Rap music is the perfect model of racial community demands, high-velocity speech, threats of retaliation if unsatisfied. A model of community demand, bad taste included, which remains an absolute right.

We wrongly disdain the strategy of demand, instead preferring the nobler, more logical combat of arguments. But to win a specific right for our community, we must add public demand for silent community-building, we must practice permanent petition, flood parliament with letters, mount a guerrilla of demands in every legal form. Other communities before us have broken governments with their relentless insistence, even in eras when it was more dangerous to stand apart. Had they meekly listened to their Leftist intellectuals, they would not be where they are now. Forget the rentiers of nationalist analysis. The anger of Europeans is an energy many covet only to squander. Their polite arguments are nothing but refusal to step onto the terrain where the right to Prefer is fought. In our discipline, only the score counts, and they have scored nothing.

Everything we think is out of reach is not any more far-fetched than what our enemies once dreamed of, and then obtained, by demanding it.

Overturning the
Adopter's Syndrome

MORE STUBBORNLY than the Left itself, civic nationalism resists racial realism, invoking what sounds like a strong argument: "A man should be judged by his deeds, not by what he is," they proudly declare. This political tendency longs for recognition, hoping for a kind of revenge, a reversed "Day of Reckoning."

Like all ideological bourgeoisies, civic nationalism believes it has a date with History. It is mistaken. It has a date with nothing. Even if it gains power, it does not make history, because it is the party of recycled methods and of "common sense." Neither is enough to alter the course of events permanently. Against ideas, values do not weigh much.

Perhaps it is for these very reasons that civic nationalism endures, persisting in aiming its efforts at slowing down projects and ideas it did not originate. At bottom, it imagines itself to be on the Right because it is opposed by the dumbest version of the Left. The Left fails to realize that civic nationalism is simply one of its own older forms. The natural movement of the Left is to dissolve social order and hierarchy, so it fails to recognize its own past incarnations and mistakes them for fascism.

Hence, whenever it nears power, civic nationalism starts recycling the Left's old ideas. To the point that its ultimate function seems to be to condemn racism in the name of Right-wing values. No matter how much it bends, accusations rain down on it as if no effort at normalization had ever been carried out.

The main positions of sovereigntism have hardly changed:

- Opposition to incoming immigration, but assimilation of those already here,

- "Judge a man by his actions, not by what he is,"

- "Real non-racism means stopping immigration" (civic nationalism belongs to the family of non-racisms),

- Fight the causes of immigration, not its consequences,

- Opposition to globalism and its cultural effects.

To many who resist the territorial invasion of the West, all this is mere intellectualized time-wasting, a vast retreat before the Rubicon of racial realism. Amusingly, racial realism actually shifts the Overton window in favor of sovereignism. Without racial realism, civic nationalism would instantly become the main enemy again for the mainstream media, which never believed for a second in its anti-racist sincerity.

In theory, racial and civic nationalism might have complemented each other, but in practice something fundamental separates them. A desire so deep that it renders them incompatible. And so civic nationalism continues to repeat its anti-racist catechism, even as its charm fades.

The smart Left knows very well that racial realism is the real danger. It is the one threat it takes seriously. Which is why it seeks to keep sovereigntism alive, offering a pseudo-Right, non-identitarian product to the segment of the public it cannot seduce, but which risks waking up to our arguments. YouTube's algorithms already perform this function, steering White audiences away from racial realism toward small-time sovereigntist peddlers like Papacito, Pierre-Yves Rougeyron, or pseudo-economists like Pierre Jovanovic.

Ironically, some Leftist intellectuals, now catching up with the consequences of immigration, seem to be drifting toward ethno-differentialist views. Twenty years from now, the idea of racially separate societies may well be a recognized current within European Leftism. At that point, I would not be surprised to find a Left which swears it never defended immigration, opposing it effectively, while a Right commits body and soul to defending the Third World.

Repeat until it's burned into your memory: civic nationalism opposes immigration inflows, but not the existing stock. The non-Whites already here? It wants to adopt them by force. Or rather, to force you to adopt them. That is what I call the adopter's syndrome, a posture halfway between Stockholm syndrome and adoption fiction.

By adopting the occupier's perspective, they rarely miss a chance to defend their sacred Palestine, though even many Maghrebis who riot in its name care little for it in reality. The Left clings to the belief that "kindness" — the refusal to hurt the other — must define immigration policy. The Right maintains its own belief in the West's infinite adoptive capacity, divorced from genetics.

Observation shows something else, something very simple: the adoption of a non-European as fully equal in importance and legitimacy to a long-rooted European is a conscious fiction between adopter and adoptee. As long as both play along and believe in the narrative, the contract holds. But it is fragile. If either side doubts, or listens to its ancestral group, the contract collapses into memory.

Everything rests on a thread: neither side must ever change its mind. But who among us has kept a single belief intact throughout life? Civic nationalism stakes its entire edifice on the fantasy that the adoptee will never shift worldview, and that the adopter will never notice disloyalty or changing behavior. Is that the conclusion of a mature mind?

The stranger within my gate,
He may be true or kind,
But he does not talk my talk,

I cannot feel his mind,
I see the face and the eyes and the mouth,
But not the soul behind.

RUDYARD KIPLING, *The Stranger*

Of course the adoptee changes as his brain develops, as his body signals his foreignness among Europeans. This alone suffices to void the contract in many cases. This is precisely one of the reasons why civic nationalism resents racial realism: our small effort effortlessly cancels their immense labor. The adoption contract usually collapses on its own, destroying civic nationalism's intellectual edifice. Look at the ruins of the reconciliation projects of the 2010s — groups like "Equality and Reconciliation" [*Égalité et Réconciliation*] now deny they ever wanted to unite native French and Maghrebi Muslims. Their wager lies scattered across the Bataclan floor and the Promenade des Anglais.

One of sovereigntism's supposedly strong arguments is that "a man should be judged by his deeds, not by what he is." This leads civic nationalism to reject blood-right citizenship, even in the face of the most alarming phenomenon of our time: the permanent settlement of low-IQ populations in the West. The moral aura of this claim makes it sound strong, but nations are not governed by morality. Nations exist only for the survival of their people. Morality applies to individuals, not peoples. To force nations to operate by a rule meant for individuals is to force them to malfunction.

Even logically, the rule collapses. Ask a civic nationalist whether a zebra, a racehorse, and a donkey should all be judged equally "by their performances," and he will call you a fool ignorant of nature. And he would be right. Yet that very principle is identical to the one we invoke to demand separate societies. To judge individuals by deeds, the average levels of performance must be comparable. That is why sports create categories. The same principle applies socially.

Populations which are poorly predisposed to respect Western standards should be judged "by their deeds"? But that is exactly why our prisons are full. And that is what they themselves complain about. They already feel treated as pariahs when judged "by their deeds." And yet the civic nationalist insists that more of the same poison will produce the antidote.

Will this century finally allow us to state calmly that Europeans are genetically better predisposed to Western civic standards than most non-Europeans? Standards like avoiding noise in public, obeying frustrating laws, respecting the rights of others, treating the opposite sex with dignity.

Consider one example: on September 9, 2005, on the French talk show *On a Tout Essayé*, columnist Christine Bravo told Pascal Gentil, a Black Olympic taekwondo champion, that her daughter, White like her, was a runner considering a professional career, but her (Black) coaches discouraged her because she was White. "You're not Black, you won't make it," she reported them saying. Silence in the studio. Pascal Gentil explained reassuringly: no need to worry, it is just genetics. White genetics are unsuited, Black genetics superior. The host laughed nervously and congratulated him. Whites have no problem accepting genetic arguments — when they cut against themselves.

In another "sport," criminality, the predispositions are governed by IQ, and thus by genetics. Perhaps Whites are also "the best" at other performances, such as life in orderly Western societies. Cue the nervous laughter and applause.

The rule "judge by deeds" must be reconsidered in the light of 21st-century science. Otherwise, the debate is mere ignorance. Scientifically correct dogma poisons this issue, mass-producing disinformed citizens. Separate societies are our inevitable destiny — if we are to have one. Diversity ideology is a pseudo-science that renders ancestral lands unlivable once they turn multiracial.

Robert Putnam, a Left-wing political scientist, found in his landmark study that diversity lowers trust — trust among citizens, trust in institutions. The myth of successful adoption should be exposed as bourgeois irrationality. If the West wishes to reach the 22nd century without catastrophic regression, it must return to rational separatism, justified by evolutionary differences. Not by contempt, but by realism.

Antispeciesism and antiracism share the same flaw: abolishing biological boundaries in the name of moral corruption, of pathological altruism. Civic nationalism's participation in the debate is pernicious. It thinks it denounces immigration with analysis and moral probity, but in truth it is only virtue-signaling in another form. In doing so, it legitimizes the anti-White Left by foregrounding their favorite theme: anti-racism.

That is why our intrusion into the debate is so unwelcome to the conventional Right. Our entire discourse cuts short what delays the arrival of separate societies, where we will never again play the role of adopting power. Civic nationalism may have been the riverbed of the French Right, but Identitarianism, or even Entitarianism, in Renaud Camus's sense, will be the waterfall's edge.

We are the 1% that must impose the intellectual climate of political, economic, and civilizational debate. The 21st century is taking the form of an hourglass, each year testing our capacity to survive. If we do not emerge with advantage, we may share the fate of the Neanderthals. The one thing we cannot waste is time. Within the next decade, as Michel Houellebecq put it, we must make White Preferism trendy.

Losing Ideas and
Charismatic Personalities

I FIND THIS process frightening. It can be so easy to ridicule a Leftist in debate that we forget the real match of ideas being played in the background. There is a tectonics of ideas, which matters far more than the victory of individuals.

Ideas fight a parallel battle of their own, with a dynamic that belongs only to them. An idea that has lost is no longer worth defending, because the public will not adopt it again for a long time, no matter what you say. Even, and especially, if they applaud you after a successful debate. Even, and especially, if they pretend to be persuaded by your words. What people say they admire and what they actually practice are two different planets.

The idea of hierarchy has suffered this fate, just as the idea of judgment has. Both have lost. We now live in a society where it is impossible to build a system of thought that includes judgment and hierarchy.

Is great music superior to a traditional djembé rhythm? Is the Ariane 5 rocket superior to Haitian voodoo magic? Does a DNA editing tool outweigh the Nambikwara recipe for curare poison? Very likely, but today it is impossible to say so. Or more precisely, it is unsayable.

Try, if you like, to argue for the superiority of Western inventions. All you will do is showcase your personal debating skills, without advancing the idea you defend by a single millimeter. The worst outcome is to win such a debate while thinking you have made your idea win. In truth, your personal victory only masks your ideological defeat.

In a system that excludes judgment and hierarchy, the competition of ideas always tilts toward equality and its ideological satellites: acceptance, openness, the primacy of the other. You will then see the most modest civilization, the least developed, the farthest removed from White achievement, win the crowd's approval almost automatically. Remember that Leftist Whites unconsciously favor whatever they perceive as inferior. "If you are an inferior, then I must value you." That is the hidden formula you would uncover if you analyzed the leftist subconscious.

Every proposal, every idea, must offer the promise of a more pleasant way of life. And the lifestyle promoted by systems of thought without judgment and with soft hierarchies has simply been judged more pleasant than the lifestyle promoted by authoritarian systems with judgment and hierarchy. It undeniably demands less effort, and it is perhaps more reassuring. But one must remember that life is made first of sensations, not of concepts. The system of thought that promises the sweetest, easiest, most gratifying sensations begins with the advantage.

Of course, non-judgment has been simmering for centuries in the cauldron of Christianity. Not judging anyone feels like a respite for the mind. No longer ranking beings in hierarchies feels like a moral rest. Judgment and hierarchy continue to operate in reality, but they are no longer welcome as intellectual components of a system of thought. If you defend their relevance in debate, you may very well win, but judgment and hierarchy as ideas will silently lose.

We must therefore replace these hard and angular notions of a not-so-distant past with something that can flow into the modern atmosphere. We have entered the era of the plane of immanence, the era without hierarchy, without rigid organization. The era of the "body without organs," that strange Deleuzian concept that prefigures a society without structure, without order. The horizontal era where everything is equal.

Of course, this is only discourse, not actual practice, but it is precisely discourse that decides which ideas may appear and be defended, and which must be banished to the catacombs. What is shameful and what may parade. For now, it is our discourse that is in the catacombs. We therefore need a discourse adapted to the plane of immanence, the plane of non-judgment. This does not mean adopting those values, but rather showing that we know how to live in the world they dominate without suffering unnecessarily for it.

Preferring is neither judging nor agreeing to dissolve oneself. Preferring is not ranking, not building hierarchies. Preferring is simply letting one's nature speak. It is conforming to a force that speaks within us and makes us act, without making us guilty actors in a culpable choice.

In an era where judging, ranking, wanting, and hierarchizing have become dangerous and unproductive, we need a mode of action that produces the same effects as hierarchy and ranking, but without giving the enemy anything to use for rhetorical aikido, without giving him a single lever to rise against us, without arousing his indignation.

By leaving him inert.

The Right's Ideo-Masochism

O N T H E Right today, two camps and two agendas coexist without understanding and perhaps even without noticing each other. On one side are the analysts, fascinated by civilizational collapse, convinced that the analytical phase is only beginning and ready to keep commenting until the very end. Confident in their numbers, they normalize the geopoliticization and hyper-intellectualization of every social issue, they scorn anything that brings debate back to the identity question, and they demand that history give them the weight that their personal experience cannot. On the other side are a handful of idea experimenters, who believe we are in the tail end of the analytical phase and replace passivity with proposals they want to be concrete and realistic. The idea of community networks belongs to this attempt. This face-off, supposedly constituting the online Right, even tries at times to unite. But between those who chase views with an analyst's mindset and those who want to speak the truth and offer solutions without being banned from social media, the split has become obvious.

This situation does not merely divide the Right, it destroys its very definition, insofar as both of these camps cannot truly be the Right at once. The false Right, obsessed above all with seeming respectable and proving its anti-racism, produces no new concepts, only new angles of analysis. It generates what we now call "content," designed to be more interesting than important, surfing anti-system themes to endlessly comment on current events. Sometimes it even attacks racial realism with more zeal than the Left itself, relentlessly working to marginalize it. This asymmetry is a major obstacle. While the Left spins its intellectual web and spreads its ethnomasochism, the ideomasochism within our circles prevents the Right from structuring its own sphere.

Faced with this sterility, can the Right overcome jealous hostility to build a Counter-Cathedral, a resonance chamber dedicated to spreading concepts? By breaking the invisibility imposed by the Left's Cathedral, we would be constructing the war machine we need. The Right-wing Counter-Cathedral would be defined by a dynamic of dialogue and mutual legitimization among creative Right thinkers, channeling their otherwise productive rivalry. Until now, the alt-right of racial realism has not engaged in this process on a large scale. It cross-references itself too rarely, with each actor behaving like an isolated entity, making little use of cross-legitimation strategies. Yet, it is impossible to impose a school of thought without this work. Conceptually, the Right behaves like a soundproof chamber, while the Left functions as a media echo chamber, a true factory for turning Leftist concepts into notables. A well-designed Right Counter-Cathedral would function like a network of competing departments within a single enterprise, with the goal of producing conceptual resonance. A notion like Legitimate Preference, for example, cannot spread beyond a small circle unless it is supported by a collective echo. If each representative of racial realism were to create a key concept, cited and highlighted by the others, we could amplify the reach of our ideas by legitimizing one another: "As the excellent so-and-so says"; "As such-and-such thinker rightly reminded us." Not to sink into parody, but to ignite a collective engine. Just as in martial arts, where the master's assistant exaggerates the force of techniques to give him prestige, we must adopt a method that the academic Left has mastered: the art of giving one another face.

But the Left is born on a slope, in ease, in laxity, it is by essence a collective, an association. The Right, by contrast, is born on an ascent, in effort, and rests on an entrepreneurial logic. Its ideas, rarer and more demanding, require long-term vision and a concrete grasp of reality. This builder's spirit recalls Ayn Rand's "Atlases," those who carry the world on their shoulders, drained by Echidna, mother of all parasitic monsters. The Right is effort, ascent, competition. Rivalry always arises within a circle of shared sympathy. A rival is someone with whom one shares common ground and ambition, but who diverges in form, an ally of our own ideological productivity. Rivalry stimulates creativity, but it also creates tensions that can weaken. A Counter-Cathedral channels this energy to make it productive, preventing it from turning into hatred born of weakness and jealousy.

If the identitarian Right values idea producers, it can break the age of commentators and project its vision into the minds of the elite. For the elite only perceives positively what has been legitimized, or what appears to have been. Since no electoral victory is as reliable as a cultural victory, why not test this strategy? To give one another face, to institutionalize our own intellectual sphere, to lend magnetism to our dark halo. My conviction today is that only this process will allow us to appear on the screens of thought, and finally to spread into the mental atmosphere of the age.

Dear Democracy

THE RIGHT stands at a bad crossroads, pulled between two paths that will not yield the outcomes we want. On one side, a poor conservatism that thinks through the rearview mirror, clinging to human nature as if it were an untouchable jewel. On the other side, an alt-right fascinated by an authoritarianism that will not lead us to a serene, unapologetic White Preference, since that very authoritarianism is justified by the racial status quo.

I want to defend a proposition that stakes everything on the technological transformation of our societies, to achieve a mixture of *dolce vita* through racial homogeneity and excellence through transhumanist enhancement. In February 2024, Jef Costello, in his review of *Legitimate Preference* on unz dot com, for which I thank him, highlighted a possible contradiction in this vision, which can seem techno-naive if one does not understand what it is answering. White Prometheanism, the engine of innovation and progress, can either illuminate or consume, depending on the hand that wields it. In my view, this depends on how one defines conservatism, because it is that definition which decides whether we gain access to genuine Progress or only to its simulacrum.

Let me clarify the point. If Legitimate Preference overturns the guilt and all the sad affects that the accusation of racism was supposed to inflict on us, Prometheanism overturns the negativity the Left has tried to pin on the fuzzy concept of capitalism. That concept has changed definition several times since its beginnings, which should discredit its credibility, or at least reveal that it is little more than an intellectual investment designed to credit you and give you face within the polite circle of right thinking.

The Prometheanism I defend is the same phenomenon turned right side up, cleared of blame and restored. From photosynthesis to predation, from fern to bear, all living things have practiced the concentration of resources through strategies of capture, which led to the emergence of the treasure of treasures, the brain. It is literally solar fire becoming thinking matter, fire that became vision after crossing the chasms of irrationality, that produced and laid upon the cold and indifferent cosmos the scintillating reason that observes the world, the thing that makes us gods in the making.

The Right should stop producing anti-capitalist critiques as if it could do better than the Left, because that ring serves only one master. Capitalism, as they deploy it, is a straw concept, a scarecrow that can only be beaten with the stick of jealousy or impotence. The Right's intellectual production would do well to notice that what the Left talks about under the word capitalism is one of its usual half-baked fantasies, poorly conceived and poorly understood.

Prometheanism could become the Right's distinctly identitarian concept, meant to set upright what the twisted and gloomy notion of capitalism pretended to curse by identifying only a late moment in its development, its phase of concentrating wealth, then knowledge, and perhaps one day, the means to make intelligence multiplanetary. We must reconcile ourselves to this impulse toward perpetual Progress and the mastery of inert matter. This is the reversal which the concept of Prometheanism contains: it stands to capitalism as Legitimate Preference stands to racism,as a verdict of innocence, a restoration, in one word, de-Leftization.

Jef Costello also raised the objection that love which justifies itself, as I justify Legitimate Preference through Prometheanism, is weaker and less legitimate than a love that needs no justification. He is right, or rather, he would be right if Legitimate Preference were love. But although we often confuse the two, this is not the case. We will certainly not love all Whites, yet we must strive to prefer all of them to other groups. To prefer Whites is to seek tirelessly to give them advantage as an in-group, not as individual persons. It is to make this question the parameter of every decision. It is the entire positive relationship that a White Preferist undertakes to maintain with the super-group to which he belongs.

In France, where any attempt at racial realism remains a fearful whisper, this debate is struggling to be born. In the United States, that kind of realism is on its native ground. The faint stirrings perceived in Italy or England may remain insufficient if no concept validates and authorizes the right to Prefer. Without a bold heading, the European Right risks flickering out, becoming either the Left's speed bump or a caricature of itself, reduced to a harder tone and harsher policing.

In this chapter, which launches the augmented edition of *Legitimate Preference*, as in the original formula, I will not try to show off before my readers. The tone I adopt is that of a practicing preacher. Once again, I shall step outside my core expertise, since I will venture onto the ground of cognitive enhancement and our constitutional framework, the framework in which we are meant to evolve throughout the 21st century, our dear democracy, allegedly the least bad of all systems, according to Churchill.

That claim has probably become false, and we are pretending nothing has changed. Much has changed. To begin with, our fellow citizens have become far more apolitical than before, and therefore far less fit for democracy, helped along in this by the presence of the Third World settled on our soil. In general, they are incapable of grasping the stakes, they embrace apoliticism as a form of salutary normality, or they reduce everything to a tax protest, which is perfectly understandable yet insufficient. Many of them, when they do vote, satisfy preferences based on surface impressions, on the physical appearance of candidates, or on childish ideals, sometimes taking an interest in their own vote only 24 hours before going to the polls. More often, others vote for civilizational transformations they would not endure for a single morning were those transformations to arrive at their door. Still others, far more numerous than we would like to think, know perfectly well that Europe is undergoing a violent invasion, but, not yet affected themselves, choose to stick to centrist habits. That is the most cowardly vote imaginable.

We are therefore entrusting the destiny of Western super-societies to peoples in cognitive decline, capable of repeating the very operation that led them to misery, denouncing the man they elected, never suspecting that they are the artisans of their own end.

We must take this problem seriously if we truly wish to continue along the democratic road. Edward Dutton sets out his worries about intellectual collapse in his magisterial book *At Wits' End* (which has been published in French, by Alba Leone, under the title *The Twilight of Intelligence*).

The much-mocked Boomers do not perform much worse in global political analysis than young Leftists, who are said to edge Rightward when they start their working life, and move firmly Rightward once they become ordinary taxpayers, since self-interest can produce Leftism among the unproductive and Rightism among those who are productive yet heavily taxed. Let us also recall the large gap between the votes of young men and young women: young women show a much stronger tendency than their male counterparts to move toward the Left, which bodes ill for the formation of future balanced White households.

With this in mind, I find myself agreeing with a well known French Leftist, the LFI deputy Aymeric Caron, who wrote in his 2017 essay *Utopia XXI*: "There is no point in allowing everyone to express themselves on all subjects and in every possible way if that expression is not qualitative. When one of my fellow citizens votes in ignorance, he harms me. A just democracy cannot allow a stupid opinion to outweigh an informed one. If that happens, it is no longer a democracy, but an idiocracy." And further: "It seems dangerous to allow everyone to vote without first verifying each person's capacity to issue a pertinent opinion."

French Right-wing circles found it wise to be scandalized by these remarks. I think it would be better to adopt them and redirect them in the service of the true Right.

Before continuing on the matter of voter responsibility, I should clarify the following. Even today, the Left's political conscience says quite explicitly that the Right should not be part of certain public debates, or be invited on television sets, on the grounds that it is not a mode of thought, but a mere affect of hatred and rejection. Style to the Right, thought to the Left — this division of roles, bequeathed by Roland Barthes and operating like a curse, must have its reversal, or rather its overturning. We must contemplate the exclusion of the Left from political debate, since it has completed its transformation into a theory of self-destruction and now amounts to nothing more than a plebiscite for putting Whites in danger. The Left has largely become the political cancer of developed societies, first and always anti-White, anti-native, anti-tradition, then anti-liberty, and finally anti-Jewish, now a tax mafia clamped like a giant tick upon its host, now a cartel of magistrates for street thugs. The Left is nothing but a slope into the West's hell. Alas, that slope lies less in the political offer than in the average voter, that Sunday cyclist who loves the most inadvisable gentle grades.

How many more decades does that voter intend to tolerate magistrates who act as the facilitators of crime? All those citizens who say they cannot stand immigration anymore, yet vote at every election so that everything continues, are like so many horizontal hanged men, strangling themselves by pulling with their own necks — no other force but their own kills them.

While we wait for cognitive enhancement to spread by mimetic desire, let us at least agree on the Right that there is a problem in entrusting our democracy to categories of voters who do not grasp the consequences of their act, and let us admit that it is less serious to scandalize a few consciences than to watch our children disappear beneath the wheels and knives of the Third World.

If we are to imagine the end of our torments, we will have to rip up the manual of democratic practice as we currently conceive it. Let us ask a simple and unprecedented question: In what sense should the vote of retirees and long-term inactives count as much as that of an autochthonous active carrying the country on his back? We face a genuine army of voters from the baby boom generation, occupied above all with enjoying their free time. Besides the fact that their vote is literally zombified by anti-racism, what justifies equality between them and the active population who produce the consumable reality?

The same question applies to anyone incapable of passing a basic test on the institutions. On what grounds should such a person be given the same electoral weight as a trained citizen, when we do not apply that logic to the rules of the road? Are democratic accidents not just as deadly as traffic accidents?

We could extend the list of questions. Should an expatriate be able to decide the fate of those who stayed in the country on the same terms as they do? Not to mention a non-European voter whose mere electoral influence literally violates the principle of Legitimate Preference.

The civic status a citizen occupies should confer a specific electoral weight. An autochthonous active should count at least twice as much as a retiree or an inactive. Yes, we have reached the point where we must choose between mastering equality or agreeing to withdraw from history. As long as such measures are not instituted, we should speak of dysfunctional democracy.

In any case, the voter who laments this situation and has himself produced it, through apoliticism, a plague on them all, a stupefying centrism, must no longer be left to his irresponsibility. The logic of voter accountability must finally be discussed without taboo. What I propose here is not the expression of technical expertise, it is the expression of naked will. What you will read undoubtedly suffers from assorted technical gaps, which can be repaired. Do not stumble over what is optional, but rather keep in mind the spirit of the democratic shock I am sketching.

The principle I want to establish, which will be opposed only by a contrary will, is to associate each voter with the effect of his vote, or of his refusal to vote. Will this be a digitized card establishing his citizen profile, as one builds the profile of an investor, or a patient through a digital file? Let the most practical measure make itself known. The essential thing is that this accountability measure finally produces voters who accept consequences.

I believe the feasibility of what follows depends on political will and on bringing the administration to heel. I believe in the shock of democratic simplification that no longer spares the very source that elects traitors, the majority of voters themselves. To be clear, this is not about creating files of behaviors that interest almost no one and are not mysterious. It is about confronting each person with concrete consequences, to repair the relationship between democracy and its users.

First, each person should vote not for a man, but for a series of measures. In such a system, a vote for ruined borders and the opening to the Third World would drastically increase your local taxes if you have chosen to live in a predominantly White area. A vote for judicial laxity and police disarmament would mean that, when you call emergency services, you will be routed to a de-escalation association or to unarmed brigades, rather than to the normal police service equipped with weapons and repressive methods. A simple identifier, like a social security number asked for at the moment of the call, coupled with an AI analyzing incoming requests, could deliver to users a service that is in accord with what they expressed at the ballot box.

It is profoundly dysfunctional that anti-fascist citizens who spray ACAB on walls and vote accordingly should still have access to the police like everyone else.

A vote to close nuclear power stations would affect your electricity bill if your power is produced by those same plants, or would require you to use only the available green energy. In short, a voter made accountable for his choices will be a far better user of democracy, because it is the de responsible voter who has brought to power the traitors and incompetents of recent decades, without ceasing to complain about them only to then reelect them.

Beyond such measures of civic coherence, we should at a minimum desire a meliorative action on the cognitive capacities of the democratic animal that we are. Two political dimensions follow: to change the nature of the Right by making it assume something it does not dare even to think, namely, that we must make human nature evolve by touching cognitive capacity, and to change the conditions of voting by accepting that some of our fellow citizens no longer meet the intellectual conditions for understanding what shapes the fate of societies. If never addressed, such irresponsibility promises the death of the West.

According to an article by Louis Maurin, director of the Observatoire des Inégalités, published in *Le Monde* on 31 August 2023, the percentage of French people who thought there were too many immigrants reached 74% in 1995, yet the leading anti-immigration party of the time won only 15%. One option is to improve marketing strategy and burnish the offer. Coming from a persuasion trade, I would gladly do so, but it will not change the nature of the crowd.

Since Gilles Deleuze, the nature of democracy itself has mutated. It is now the instrumentalization of the majority in the service of minority rights. The real purpose of our societies is to be stable, prosperous, and busy with creating their own challenges, not fetishizing words whose dead meanings no longer matter to anyone.

There is also the volatility of political opinion. In my militant life, I have seen a recurring phenomenon that extends far beyond my personal observation. Many people, absolutely convinced by an identitarian diagnosis, change their vote at the last minute for poetic reasons. Jean Lassalle is the example, a representative of rural France by his shepherd's look, almost communist in his ideas, yet able to seduce a nostalgic electorate trapped in the habit of a vote without real meaning. "At least he is not one of those bureaucrats, he knows the real life of us ordinary people." In 2022, he won 3.1% of the vote, more than a million voters, often rural Frenchmen dreaming of an older France (*Le Monde*, April 11, 2022). They vote for him thinking they are defending their identity, while his positions, favoring a Left universalism, work against the Remigration they claim to want.

This is not an isolated case. Studies show that 40% of French voters modify their choice in the final days before the vote, often under the sway of emotions or vague promises (IFOP, 2022). This inconsistency, which I have observed many times, reflects a deeper sickness, a growing incapacity to select a program that truly protects our societies.

We must also note that many Whites in France, probably centrists, live Preference by proxy, delegating it. They grant their Jewish fellow citizens an importance far greater than they grant their own group, they worry about their safety and about anything that might threaten it, as if those lives were worth twenty times their own. Thus, the security of Israel, important though it is strategically, seems to them immeasurably more important than the security of Whites in South Africa, despite the atrocities inflicted on them by Blacks with an average IQ of 70. Their very perception of reality has been damaged to the point that the defense of their own identitarian interests has become a scandal in their own eyes.

Taboo and evident truth become entangled the moment we try to connect omnicriminality with the presence of the Third World. The penetration of multiracial society has gone so deep that the link between the two may no longer even be thinkable for many voters. We have accepted major electoral dysfunctions by filing them under the label of freedom. If Spinoza called the will of God a refuge of ignorance, the sacred freedom of the voter may have become the refuge of incompetence.

If these remarks I'm permitting myself appear violent, it is not only to protest against a dead-end no one is denouncing, but also because they fit logically with our short term technological horizon, that of neuroenhancement. I'll add that raising the intelligence of individuals is not authoritarianism imposed out of a taste for control, but rather is a liberation offered out of necessity, like a parent who educates without any pleasure in domination, whereas authoritarianism cherishes the yoke for its own sake.

Research in neuroenhancement is advancing rapidly. Brain computer interfaces, such as those developed by Neuralink, already make it possible to improve cognitive functions. According to a Neuralink report from January 2024, a tetraplegic patient was able to control a cursor by thought with unprecedented precision. Elon Musk has declared (in an interview with *Wired* in 2024) that we can amplify human capacities

beyond biological limits, not to enslave, but to free the potential of each person. Already tested in medical cases, this technology could tomorrow optimize memory or analytical comprehension, making each person more capable of grasping the complex stakes of society. Imagine a voter able to decode economic or migratory mechanisms without drowning in the typical disinformation of dissidence. Neuroenhancement offers that clarity, not as a luxury, but as a remedy for electoral inconsistency.

Of course, the general public could reject cognitive enhancement if it is presented without a communication strategy. Such a proposal, if poorly presented, would be perceived as an insult to collective intelligence, one more technocratic diktat, especially in a climate of distrust where 62% of French people refuse technological implants (IFOP, 2021). The solution, which I will not elaborate here, may be to reverse the perception: rather than an assault on their intelligence, a chance to free themselves from the chains of habitual smoke and mirrors. Technocrats thrive on citizens' incomprehension, manipulating stakes they know are opaque. By making each person able to pierce that opacity, neuroenhancement would end that exploitation. We now know that an enlightened people still lets itself be deceived by hollow promises. What we need is an augmented people. Otherwise, only elites in their own image will ever emerge from this poor people.

So, this is not about advocating something scandalous and disconnected from what is technically possible, it is about becoming the political pole that announces and desires this cognitive enhancement, and links it to its political corollary in an adult and consistent way. Those who drag their feet on transhumanist matters should be treated like children and dreamers. We, the White Promethean Right, must add this theme to the Preferist balance, to credit ourselves by anticipating what is coming. And the best way to announce this change, which to some has the look of cybernetic daydreaming, is to present it as inevitable.

Of Private Space —
Liberalism and Identity

A T THE VERY moment when the population is slowly beginning to realize that every form of socialism impoverishes, and that the redistribution of wealth means nothing other than the seizure of our personal resources, the young digital Right advances the claims of "Nicolas who pays" — the 30-year-old White worker who has no right to anything except to shut his mouth and be plundered by the State. From this starting point, this genuinely new Right demands a solidarity, albeit less suicidal in economic terms, with certain retirees enjoying high pensions, people who voted socialist all their lives. In other words, it demands a cut to the huge pensions of those who voted anti-racist all their lives, and it couples this with the denunciation of the "Karims of the *banlieues*," symbolized by the image of a hostile North African adolescent involved in the economy of crime, clad in the uniform of a thug that makes him look like a homosexual forced to permanently wear a tracksuit.

The association of these two groups of ideas — the right to enrich oneself through work without being robbed by an incompetent State, and the identification of the identitarian problem posed by the invasion we are undergoing — forms a supposedly contradictory set. In other words, liberalism, which contains within it every desire for personal enrichment along with suspicion of the State's expansion, would by nature be opposed to the goal of the identitarian militant, which is to obtain a homogeneous society composed of White Europeans.

Liberal society does indeed privilege one value, freedom, and one scale of humanity, the individual. But the individual has no other gods than the interest of his immediate circle, not even his own personal interest as anti-liberals imagine, and it is rarely in his immediate interest to confront the crowd with its rumors and its accusations of racism. And yet, when Africa spills over, only what the Left calls "racism," in reality Preferism, constitutes the antidote. For a Frenchman, this is strikingly counterintuitive.

Whether expressed in polished or vulgar terms, "racism" springs from an aristocratic sentiment, a sentiment that delights in confronting the lazy and false opinion of the crowd. If aristocracy means anything, it means standing against the tearful sentiment of unconditional welcome. It will therefore always be in tension with the liberal proposition that leaves it up to each person to decide whom he'd like to see from his window and who crosses his threshold.

The point I wish to make is this. It is precisely the tension between the liberal sentiment, which otherwise dries up when it governs alone, and the lofty aristocratic demand that provides the mechanism for the Right we wish to bring forth. The two appear contradictory, but in reality they form a single body, head and legs joined, if one accepts the natural hierarchy between the continuation of Identity and personal enrichment. Identity is the head, enrichment the legs.

Thierry Marx, the Michelin starred chef often invited on French television, shows us by his indifference to Europe's biological identity how the business-only perspective functions. Whether he is driven by passion for work or for money, if the identitarian vision is absent from his thought, the outcome will be much the same, Africa will spill directly into the restaurant's kitchens. Only the disruption of the economy that will follow, because it will follow, will be noticed as a problem.

There must therefore be a constraint from the outside to prevent the non-identitarian restaurateur from becoming an agent of invasion, however sympathetically liberal he may be. To reject invasion without becoming poor, to grow rich without dissolving, this requires an aristocratic elite to set the conditions of this ideal: teaching biological Identity and admitting it into political reflection, rejecting anti-system diversion, educating toward responsible voting. Indeed, this is one of the first goals of Legitimate Preference.

Pursuing this line of thought, we see how it collides with the very notion of public space from an angle the mainstream has left unexamined, the relation between the common good and the dilution of identity. Legitimate Preference itself implies reducing the portion of pre-programmed politics contained in the notion of public space. If space is truly public, it cannot bend to identitarian requirements, and if it is fully identitarian, it is no longer truly public, since an unspoken clause limits its use to the Euro-descendant user, a shareholder of European identity.

Since that clause is unspeakable in France, even unthinkable, there must be strong borders. But this situation forces the border to compensate for what political thought refuses to do, to think exclusivity, or to constitutionalize Legitimate Preference. And the power of the border rests on the electoral success of the Right, which makes its effectiveness fragile.

Let us be clear, the migratory invasion manifests itself in public space. Africans with identity cards fill certain places, all of them public, disrupting overall cohesion and even corrupting private spaces by sheer proximity. To be identitarian today is therefore simply to desire or seek their absence. This is an unconscious way of seeking spaces protected from public space. In practice, when public space reveals its true identity, it becomes "living together." And when the user finds himself paying more to enjoy calm, he teleports into a private zone, whether a White one or one that is discretely privatized by the cost of entry.

Public space and the dwindling of Whites thus end up coinciding when Legitimate Preference can no longer be thought. Reestablish borders, yes, of course, but that depends on fragile and laborious electoral success. The Right may eventually win, but the electoral pendulum will relativize every hard-won gain.

Therefore, we must consolidate the mother of all floodbanks, the moral authorization given to citizens to practice Legitimate Preference, by constitutionalizing it. But even that measure is only a formula unless an obscure intellectual elite, derided and mocked even within the so-called "dissidence," plays the role of icebreaker and snowplow, breaking the ice of respectable opinion and clearing the snow of parasitic ideas. Then it must tell the masses the conditions for obtaining individual enrichment without identitarian death, the multiplication of contractual spaces.

To put it simply, this is the spirit of the free cities, or rather, cities freed from "living together" by a certain kind of contract, explicit or implicit, but resurrected in modern form. Of course, we will not relive Lübeck, the head of the Hanseatic League in the 13th century, nor Florence. We must forge our own models. Yet, Monaco provides something of an example of a modernized free city. Without ever pronouncing the forbidden words, Monaco has achieved an identity by attracting foreign capital and implicitly selecting its residents by wealth, which serves, for now, as an anti-Third World and anti-Leftist filter.

It seems we have no other options for the moment than two caricatures of the future: the medical and demographic deserts of empty regions, or the social fortresses of ultra-expensive neighborhoods, the only places where, by chance or by price, more or less White enclaves still form. Between vacuity and inaccessible luxury, bewildered Whites await permission to reinvest their identity in daylight. The strategic horizon should therefore be to combine identitarian consciousness with material accessibility. But to precipitate that construction, the progressive privatization of certain spaces and the voluntary association of users who share the same identity may be the only real levers for escaping the impasse.

Generalized apoliticism on the part of people who abandon themselves to comfort and short-term thinking, as well as on the part of the elites who refuse to name the exclusivity required, has led to the soft, non-identitarian notion of "public space." Once a place where collective identity was expressed, it has become the place where White identity cancels itself, confirming the Republic in its belief that its particularism is its universalism. This might still go on for a long time, but the survival of White peoples will not endure it indefinitely.

The conclusion is that we must identify the various hatreds of private property that disguise themselves as economic theories, for they systematically destroy resistance to migratory invasion. Anti-liberalism and anti-capitalism have their own gravitational pull and work toward no end other than themselves. Anyone on the Right who embraces them edges towards anti-Westernism and feeds passions that shrink and shrivel our Promethean drive.

Contractual law, recognized and enforceable, provides the legal basis for organizing these distinct spheres where users define the conditions of their coexistence. These contractual spaces, these free cities, do not violate the principle of freedom, they apply it by giving control of thresholds and of belonging back to individuals. By invoking private law, we set against the fiction of a universal public space the strongest legal reality, the freedom of association and of contract.

We would only be at the beginning of our troubles if no social and economic revolution were to come. I write here at the limit of what I can formulate, trying not to fall into the description of a fantasized horizon. It is in this reorientation, from undifferentiated public space to assumed private space, that lies the key to a true cultural and identitarian reconquest.

The Bathroom Ideology

M AKING "TRENDY" what Houellebecq has unfortunately dubbed "White supremacism" is one of the most crucial battles for our cause. In truth, "supremacism" boils down to nothing more than the right to celebrate ourselves and to envision our lineage stretching into the future. To win that fight, we can no longer appeal straight to people's intellects, the fortress of their already calcified conclusions.

From what I've seen in the slow grind of shifting opinions, people do change their minds. But it follows a sly cycle: observation, doubt, and the quiet erosion of certainties. It's a far cry from cold logic.

These shifts don't come from airtight arguments. They spring from something more personal and gut-level: self-interest.

When virtue-signaling clashes with self-interest, self-interest always wins. That's ironclad.

In this chapter, I'll try to lay out what could evolve into a right-wing political communication strategy.

Take a striking example of the dynamic I'm talking about. When Europeans wake up, often through sheer comparison, to how shockingly low their standard of living is compared to Americans in the same social bracket, or to the wealthiest Europeans (say, Norwegians), it might spark a subtle pivot in their views.

The change isn't flashy. But it shows that you can chip away at their bedrock economic beliefs over time.

From that simple spark, a full-blown questioning can ignite. It often leads to ditching the entire "ideological package" they grew up with or just drifted into by default.

In my experience, women are the quickest to flip like this. I could be off base, but they strike me as more attuned to material comparisons and the pull of a better life, enough to rethink their ideological stances with surprising ease.

Especially when they clock how everyday household gadgets in uninhibited capitalist countries (ones that don't blush at their White identity) are not just highly desirable but way more attainable than in places steeped in atmospheric socialism.

The over-the-top bathroom sticks in my mind as a prime case.

Alongside the kitchen, it's one of the home features that matter most to women. Sure, other high-tech appliances play a starring role too, as emblems of cutting-edge living.

Men have gotten hooked on certain gadgets as well. But what I'm getting at here isn't just the lure of stuff. It's how what those objects represent seeps into our ideological habits.

In the end, it doesn't matter if bathrooms and kitchens really hold that emotional and practical punch, greater, in my view, than other fixtures. The key is this: having or lacking modern comfort gear screams whether you're a winner or a loser. And that makes it a hell of a lever for flipping opinions.

Here's how I frame my hunch: Handing over a sleek new kitchen or a luxury bathroom is probably the most persuasive proof of love a man can give. It's not mere gift-giving. It's a flex of status, prosperity, and attentiveness to home life, qualities that score big in any household.

I suspect it's these everyday, gut-deep details that can rattle ideological certainties. Picture a woman realizing that Whites of her own class in techno-capitalist societies enjoy more practical and plush household setups. These seemingly trivial observations can kick off a questioning spiral that ends up reshaping the whole family.

In my book, this process rarely bubbles up to full awareness. That's exactly what makes it work, its half-buried status as an under-the-radar insight. Full-blown awareness would trigger mental or emotional pushback, rousing those dormant convictions. That's why cross-aisle political debates, by tripping moral alarms, make real ideological turnarounds all but impossible.

Gentle Envy: The Hidden Engine of Change

That envious side-eye at the "American cousin" or the Scandinavian citizen (so often hailed as a model in France) works its magic quietly. It downplays the ideological baggage. By fading out theoretical clashes, it lulls the egalitarian fervor that fires up Europe's old-school socialists. The shift happens without feeling like a betrayal of their core ideals. This smooth, opposition-free glide carves out room for deep evolution with no visible pain.

That leads to a clear takeaway: It's way more effective to spotlight hard, concrete lifestyle gaps between Right-leaning and Left-leaning countries (with France as the neo-communist benchmark) than to drone on with abstract theory. Numbers, solid facts, and eye-catching visuals hit straight at people's wants and dreams. Intellectual arguments, meanwhile, just bounce off entrenched beliefs or feed defensive reflexes.

The human brain chases its own gain: meeting needs, chasing comfort, upgrading life conditions. In that light, visions of a "techno-paradise" pull like gravity on every mind, especially when middle age rolls in without owning a home or any shot at one. Right then, buried cravings turn into rocket fuel. They crack open profound doubts that would've seemed unthinkable just years before.

Sure, it's on us regular folks, our life choices, our votes, if those personal wins don't materialize. And the Left's stroke of genius is convincing us that our discomfort stems from injustice. But we're not after some inner Right-wing faith from them. We want practical allegiance, hooked on real, immediate perks.

The opinion-shift cycle we need to nurture could easily run through desirable objects, to reach those who crave them, especially the women.

This isn't just smart tactics. It's strategic emergency. The reason to elevate constant progress to quasi-religious status (what I call Prometheism) is the showdown with a rival faith: Islam.

With demographics soon pushing past 2 billion adherents, its spread poses a short-term strategic threat our side wildly underrates.

Islam, for all the nonsense in its doctrine and the Stone-Age vibe of its rituals, actually seduces some Right-wing intellectuals. Philippe Baillet unpacks this at length in his book *The Other Third Worldism*.

Why? It dangles the promise of dominance, a balm for mediocre men, and a long-term lure for the coldest cynics. This raw pledge of pleasure hooks both the "rationalizers" and the true believers. Its blunt pitch, "Enjoy twice: once on earth by lording over infidels, once in heaven watching them roast from paradise," exploits two core frailties of the modern West:

1. The emasculation of White European men.

Weary, weakened, and severed from their roots, they might end up submitting to Islam not out of belief, but exhaustion. It's a dodge from conflict, a survival nod to conquest.

That's François in Houellebecq's *Submission*. That's what Western European peoples are doing. That's what traitor Keir Starmer is engineering.

2. The virility of White dissidents.

On the flip side, White men virile enough to rebel against the Left's democratic blackmail might get drawn to Islam's macho, conquering image. They could convert for convenience or a craving for hierarchy lost in their own societies. Or just to snag sexually appealing *"beurettes"* (young North African women hunting European partners). That's the pitch from communist Alain Soral, via his anti-Jewish, pro-Islam outfit Equality and Reconciliation.

These two currents, total opposites on the surface, could ironically brew the same disaster: a surge of male conversions to Islam in coming decades. Submissive guys and opportunistic converts would make a toxic brew for the West's future.

If that's not convincing, just watch: A whole nation might be ful-filling Houellebecq's prophecy from *Submission* right before our eyes: England.

The British PM isn't doing anything but orchestrating his coun-try's willing surrender to Islam's conquest phase in the UK.

Barring a brewing revolt, this capitulation spells tech regression and squandered chances for the nation.

In that scenario, women stand to lose the most from creeping Islamization. Little White English girls, tortured, raped, and mur-dered by Pakistani criminals, bear brutal witness.

Any self-respecting Westerner wishes hell on those monsters. But other men exist, and they're legion.

Whether spineless or swaggering, plenty could slot right into an Islamic order. Women would lose freedoms, rights, and the status they now take for granted.

I bet they're not ready to forfeit what feels like the hard-won legacy of feminism's better fights: their liberties and the comforts tech modernity delivered.

Their brand of resistance, less combative than men's, fits our era's fake gospel of amplifying the "oppressed."

I know full well that bogus regressive feminists and a political mob cover for Third World crimes in the West, crimes gutting White flesh, fate, and genes.

I'm not claiming women or feminism alone can fix our mess by some innate magic.

What I am saying: If there's a machine for churning out joyful identitarians, it starts by wooing women with Prometheism's gadgets.

Only once they're hooked on its tech fruits, immunized against Third Worldism and, in a sense, "born again" in identitarian empow-erment, can they unleash that breezy, sexy lightness to smash every dam we target.

Picture the suggestive power of a squad of young, hot identitarian influencers, all-in on the cause of Legitimate Preference. They chat it up freely, with laughs and zero hang-ups. Imagine desirable, popular young women breezily owning positions flat-out incompatible with Islam. Women making it crystal clear they'll only vibe with White guys who share their views and their WOD outlook (White Only Dating), which, let's remember, is totally legal.

Some heroines are already doing it, with TikTok dances taunting the far Left.

Who would argue that the persuasive pull of beautiful, desirable White women can hawk cars but not ideas?

The Left's venomous jabs would just amp up the thrill of Right-wing showmanship. Every identitarian militant would clock the shift in a heartbeat: The winds have changed. A new social norm is here, theirs.

This vision feels like pie-in-the-sky next to the sludge spreading under our noses. But it's also an emerging reality we need to stage for viral takeoff.

People love saying women lack deep political convictions, that they just echo their husbands or their bubble. But that glosses over a sharper truth: When women embody a vision, they make it seductive, irresistible even, to anyone chasing their favor.

Loads of Right-wing young women size up societies with clear-eyed pragmatism: Which ones promise the best shots and a truly fulfilling life?

For many, it's unthinkable that men with a pinched worldview, inferior to ours, could claim the helm of advanced societies. They rightly see that setups ruled by backward visions, like the *homo islamicus* mindset, offer zero appealing future.

Any future forecast tips a scale with two pans. Islam's already weighing down one, whispering to mediocre, feeble Whites. The other pan needs desirable young women ready to play hardball:

Want sex, a family, affection? Sign up for the "religion" of relentless progress. That means banning Islam and every regressive throwback.

No silent signal packs more punch than the male gaze settling this: Which side has the smart, cool, pretty White girls? Time to say it out loud: The *homo islamicus* falls woefully short in offering a thriving worldview.

His patience and faith thrive on a bone-deep hatred of real life and a fetish for some pie-in-the-sky afterlife. These twin poisons, an obsession with death and a loathing for whatever makes life worth living, pulse at the heart of this religion of neutered manhood: neutered by fear, hate, and endless irrational backslide.

Through their gatekeeping of social and cultural models, women quietly build buy-in and shield the values that secure a prosperous tomorrow. Those who can spot societies delivering comfort, stability, and personal flourishing should anchor our comms strategy.

A strategy that boils down to unspoken blackmail:

Modern bathroom + high-tech kitchen + steady guys + safety = techno-capitalist society + Legitimate Preference.

This setup skips the lectures for a crisp, tempting equation. It ties instant material cravings to the societal blueprint that delivers them. If this dynamic holds, and I'm dead certain it does, then rethinking women's role and image in our doctrinal outreach is make-or-break. They might just be the opinion-flip key we're hunting.

Sure, the political Paganism I mentioned earlier makes for a textbook counterpunch. But flesh is weak, and it'll heed self-interest's call first. Only then can we supercharge Prometheism's converts into lineage loyalists.

By zeroing in here, showing them that a world of tech, demographic steadiness, and rock-solid values is flat-out better, we won't just win buy-in. We can forge a real gut-revulsion against the most radical regressive threat in 1,400 years.

The Dilemma

THE NATIONAL camp generally recoils from the stark simplicity of the Identitarian line. It strikes them as too blunt. Too indifferent to history and culture. Preferring Whites feels both aggressive and threadbare to them. So threadbare that it barely seems to engage our intelligence.

This light-traveling approach comes off as unaristocratic. And besides, they've never had much stomach for uttering forbidden words. That quickly breeds a deep disdain and a dark jealousy toward the "racists" we're supposed to be. So, thinking they've landed the knockout punch, civic nationalists sometimes hit us with this (bogus) dilemma: "Would you rather have a nice, smart Black neighbor, or a dumb, dishonest White one?"

A neighbor isn't nothing. It's enough to make a fence-sitter pause, tempted to leap too quickly to human groups' incompatibility.

I have to admit, like all my kin, I started by underrating this question. I saw it as some sleazy setup, a badly framed query. But there's a real weight to it that we can't just swat away, or we'll end up peddling some utopian pipe dream.

It's about the sheer impossibility of fully applying a doctrine's prescriptions in the grit of daily life.

Even, and especially, a doctrine our reason fully buys into. That's what I want to unpack in this short chapter, which aims to spotlight the constraints the Preferist stance demands of us.

The question irks us, probably because it only seems dumb on the surface. Though it pretends to probe our insight, it really tests our grip on discipline. The first time I heard it, a civic nationalist was springing it as a trap on a young Identitarian. A query meant to say, "See? Pure biological identity is an unworkable ideal."

What we need to grasp right off is this: Every ideal is unworkable. And we think we know why it has to be that way.

I've since seen this question resurface often as the supposed debate-ender on race as a criterion.

Sure, from a pure rhetorical angle, we could just gut its relevance by slapping back with a broader, sharper one: "If you're White yourself and have to move to a neighborhood where you know no one and nothing except its racial makeup, would you pick a Black one, Latino one, North African one, or White?"

Then there's how this question smuggles in the everyday sense of our key word, "prefer." "Which neighbor will you prefer?"

As we saw in the last chapter, the Preference we aim to enforce isn't just individual sentiment or passive Preference. It's active Preference as well.

That means actively seeking advantages for our genetic group. It's calmly letting Storge dominate Agape in practice...

Storge covers clan bonds, the love and friendship ties of the extended family.

Agape is the tyranny of selfless, unconditional love. Love with no *quid pro quo*, no logic, no feeling, bureaucratic love.

Relegitimizing Storge won't come from asking permission.

Pushing our definitions and nudging the meanings of words our way demands, as we've already said, constant vigilance in a war of words. Plus real intolerance for rival readings, the way Lhe left does it routinely. The stakes are reshaping what our sparring partner loads into certain key terms. We are repeating this here only to treat it as settled.

Finally, on pure logic, it's obvious: This question sneaks a collective-scale problem into a tidy individual pickle. Beyond the fact that no one can promise that "nice, smart Black" won't cause neighbor headaches, what's in it for us to live hemmed in by "nice and smart" stand-ins for the group replacing us? Framed that way, the issue clears up. Are we doomed to endless displays of White niceness and racial self-denial? No, of course not. But that's just the rhetorical top layer. And we'd be fools to stop there, as we'll see.

Such comebacks only ping abstract intelligence. They miss emotion, moral sentiment, that ideological heroism vibe so vital for many Whites.

The total antithesis of anti-racist morality (which demands nothing beyond lip service), Legitimate Preference only lives if it means constraints and rules for its adherents.

Yet daily life throws up serious roadblocks to even our most rational self-imposed rules.

So why stick to strict precepts if they're not fully doable?

Before moving on, let me quickly recap Hamilton's rule as a benchmark. It probes why altruistic behaviors exist in nature, where the cost to the actor often runs high. In our example, that "high cost" is putting up with an unlivable White neighbor.

Hamilton's rule answers by stressing the need to favor (select for) our closest genetic kin when deciding who reaps the upside of our risk-taking, which can stretch to self-sacrifice. In other words, from a genetic-interest angle. Geneticist J. B. S. Haldane put it this way: "I'd gladly lay down my life to save four of my grandchildren or eight of my first cousins!"

How can these basics clarify the dilemma thrown at us here?

For our personal will to swallow an ideal's constraints, even if they stretch just a bit beyond our solo limits, we need a bigger stake than our own skin in the game. The individual sacrifice has to pay off for our genetic family's scale. Otherwise, consent just won't happen.

You may have noticed: Some wildly popular dogmas oddly mismatch the moral horsepower of the folks they're pitched to. They dangle (or shove) an ideal that solo effort can't touch. And that's no accident. The sneaky goal of this "overkill" demand is reshaping our nature over time, birthing a new personality type. A fresh stubbornness, a new grit, all aimed at forging a novel human breed.

Human nature isn't some fixed god. It bends in ways we miss, thanks to the timescales involved. But the big moral principles which humanity sets for itself might just aim to tweak that deep nature, steering our evolution.

If human races are ongoing speciation in motion, then jumping in to shape that process makes perfect sense.

Whether we morph into Prometheans or dead-end abortions hangs partly on how rigorously we uphold our principles.

Yes, you have to Prefer (not love) a dumb White over a smart Black, even if it means a lousy neighbor setup, whenever you can swing it. That's the will we need, even if you don't do it every time. Because it's a practice that sharpens racial-ship awareness.

It's also smart for us to handle our own troublemakers, skipping illegitimate loyalties the second relational friction hits. The weak links among our own must get tamed by us, staying full members of the whole we claim to want to be better.

On another note, a lurking question pops up: Should we respect a decent non-White, granting personal esteem or friendly feelings even if they're not rooted in Legitimate Preference?

Hell yes.

But Preference isn't in that league at all. It targets something else entirely. It's wiping the personal plane for the genetic one. Erasing immediate reality for the overarching good of what we've called our racial ship.

Any loyalty sparked in the heart — on sympathy circles, pure meritocracy, shared toil (in a racially mixed crew), joint sacrifice, common traits, or mutual passions — carries its own legitimacy and logic. We can't lowball that.

But all can clash with Legitimate Preference, stirring up a kind of illegitimate nation inside us. Every Preference, in that sense, is a nation seed.

The sympathy circles we all nurture with various folks feel utterly natural, utterly legitimate to us. Still, each one can potentially rival Legitimate Preference if not grounded in it.

So, Legitimate Preference acts like internal legislation, springing from our racial-ship belonging. It orders us to bench any rival Preference. That order feels harsh if you miss what it's guarding. But what the question above first teaches us is the pecking order between our everyday "illegitimate nations"—those routine loyalties—and the top moral code for a woke White: his extended family's interest.

What it secondarily shows is that daily life will inevitably chuck some event at us that makes that duty near impossible, even if we buy in fully. What matters is willing to stick to it, grasping that this ideal aims to upgrade our long-haul nature. A sharper knack for Legitimate Preference is the ticket for the European type to eventually birth the overman Nietzsche craved, the *Homo Prometheus*.

In sum, embracing this life rule can't be so rigid that it wrecks our days and benches us from duty. But it can't slack off so much that it costs us nothing. A principle meant to steer our genetic fate can't be total cozy on the personal front. Because if its short-view logic holds up, its long-view one is sacred.

The Five Sins of Wasted Time

I N THIS chapter, I'll try to draw on a brief spat I had with a French YouTuber, using it to spotlight thought habits I see as downright harmful if we want to make it anywhere near an ideological win.

Do we even want that? That's for you to mull over on your own.

Of course, my sparring partner might have wised up since then, and I'd count that as great news.

Early 2024 saw a clash with a Right-wing, anti-racist YouTuber who'd blown up during the Covid crisis with his readings and podcasts. Sporting a handle that apes the famous Identitarian YouTuber Lapin Taquin (now rebranded Lapin du Futur), he's the sovereigntist flip side to that coin. He pops up on social media with a cute little fox avatar. A solid mic, texts read slow and steady, a smooth voice, all wrap him in this wise-yet-committed persona that hooks plenty of fans. His command of YouTube's playbook, the polish and steady output on the platform (miles beyond what I've managed), earn him the tag "the YouTuber" here.

He couldn't stomach a critique I'd tossed onto the low-key Telegram channel for Legitimate Preference, so he fired back with a 40-plus-minute revenge video dedicated to me.

But when I floated a live debate against him, he clammed up fast, ducking behind our fame gap as an excuse to bail. That dodge birthed the riposte you'll find below, a way to harness the crowd's thirst for beef and push a vital idea.

First off, I have to own up that my initial critique, the one that lit the fuse, was pointlessly rude, banged out in a huff.

But I stand by its core, which is fully warranted and blasts the sterile, soul-crushing loop of analytical Right-wingery. Every fresh influencer, hungry for eyeballs, reboots questions others chewed over before, only to watch them recycled after.

In this spot, I zeroed in on a young centrist's testimony, gutted by his woke sister, aired on the YouTuber's channel. Her ironclad activism was shattering the family.

The kid laid it out blind to the punch. His sister's sectarian intolerance worked like a charm to bend the clan to her ideological whims. He wrapped by vowing open arms for his nutjob sibling if she snapped back to sanity.

A playbook I wouldn't wish on anyone aiming for actual victory.

Every argument unpacked in the riposte below strikes me as a textbook "lost opportunity" ideologically, the way New Age woo-woo spells medical doom against cancer. Time being the one thing White Identitarians can least afford to squander in this world, I want to lay out why we must do the dead opposite of what my counterpart preached.

As I reread these lines pre-publication, François Bousquet has dropped a book on anti-White racism to prove the beast exists. That rare flash of clarity and guts still falls short of what we need to dodge the fate those replacement charts forecast for every European country, given each one's demographic tipping points. That's why I keep hammering the same Preferist message from fresh angles and entry ramps.

All to arm you, my fellow Preferist preacher, with a toolkit of persuasion.

Though it started personal, this dust-up mirrors a structural rot at the Right's core. It needs to regroup for rebuilding White in-group space, not endless yakking. I boil down these lost shots to five sins of wasted time, aimed at a camp I dub here the analytical Right, the values Right, or sovereigntism, all over online spaces, with this YouTuber as Exhibit A.

1. Defeat by "Common Sense"

In his lengthy comeback video, one key idea got hammered home was: the supremacy of family over political activism.

He frames anything that might threaten it as absurd radicalism, especially hardcore political militancy. And who could challenge the rock-solid wisdom of that?

I'm afraid I have to. On the Right, we fancy ourselves the party of reclaimed common sense. Of ideas set right-side up.

We're dead wrong. Common sense only wins us claps from an audience that needs soothing, but should be sweating bullets.

First off, let's eye the poverty of this common sense, steering us through the abstraction park of our hoary Right-wing hobbyhorses.

By airing on his Right-wing channel with over 100,000 sub-scribers a testimony primed to make that family's mess worse (if the woke sister stumbles into this public laundry-washing), our YouTuber torpedoed his own principle without even clocking it: I'd struggle hard to reconcile with my brother if I caught wind that a far-Right YouTube channel with 100,000 followers had splashed his story everywhere.

Driven by the very political activism he ripped apart, our YouTuber didn't even notice that dropping his video, by its mere exis-tence, he whipped up exactly the monster he hoped to nail.

What a shame that critique can prove as tricky as the art it targets.

But that blindspot contradiction has the upside of dragging the question of unworkable values into the light, those born from "com-mon sense."

Scratch beneath the skin of fake obviousness, and we quickly find ways to trip up our starting assumptions.

Should family, the core kernel of the nation, take priority over the political resistance that grips us all? Which one bows out, which one leads, and by what rule do we sort our actions when they clash?

To answer with street-level smarts, just recall the split between politics and the political.

Politics is the tame game of opinions on the best way to run things, opinions molded by the day's intellectual fads. The political, though, is the raw eruption of clashing interests, a force that bursts out uninvited. The first you can hush to keep Christmas vibes intact, but the second slips out of every leash. Especially in family setups, where depending on the wiring, it can brew the political conflict itself.

So family, by its very nature, stands dead opposite a politics-free safe haven. But can we at least train ourselves to dodge in-family scraps? As folksy common sense seems to beg itself.

Alas, no dice again.

Your personal moral choices, sincere as hell, only bind you and leave you naked against your relatives' picks. The testimony our YouTuber aired, the one propping his botched takeaway, proves it in spades: Clashing interests don't need your buy-in, and your hush or opt-out won't kill it. It drafts you anyway.

Family, with its high-stakes freight, turns, as nearly everyone knows firsthand, into prime turf for political conflict to flare.

Separate from opinion squabbles, which you can indeed mute more often.

And above all, family splits into two clear-cut realities. Before judging and ranking the thing we're sorting, it'd help to know if the word we're wielding is one-meaning or slippery: The upward family (parents and forebears) and the downward one (kids and grandkids) play like two different beasts. When interests collide across those branches, ducking out means stabbing your own lineage in the back.

Your woke sister votes far Left, and you're a Eight-wing parent? She's backing a side itching to spring violent crooks ASAP, aiding a Third World influx that kills, rapes, beats, robs. She's in on devaluing Whites to the max. Voting to drill sexual deviancy into your kids from day one. To hand the reins to woke tyranny and the harshest tax yoke ever.

That's no idle opinion. It's a vote with heavy fallout. Wouldn't it make sense to roll out the discipline we use on our own kids when they cross lines, namely, punishment? Instead of flinging open arms and forgiving? Which tactic will your counterpart get? Which one clicks for you? Which one burns the most time for you and yours?

A clued-in Preferist knows family circles can spark these clashes sometimes and rolls with the risk.

Weighing that, we can now ask which family ends up tougher: the one that faces facts and gears up, or the one lulled by pie-in-the-sky principles from our gullible common sense?

2. Celebrating Tolerance, or How to Open Minds and Close Futures

By hyping a Right that would snatch the turf of tolerance from the Left, against a "progressivism" sunk into woke intolerance, this YouTuber pitches a strategy: notability through debate and "open-mindedness."

This delusion spawns a massive strategic blunder. Nassim Nicholas Taleb, in his article "The Most Intolerant Wins," nailed an unyielding truth, backed by hard science: The big wins, whether political, cultural, or ideological, always go to the rigid crew, those who dictate terms without entertaining debate. The tolerant? They inherit defeat and squeaky-clean morals. The same moral smugness that blinds them to tragedy. "The most intolerant wins" isn't just an article title, it's the literal lesson we must swallow. Peddling tolerance means ditching long-term payoff for instant social pats on the back. Letting go of the bird in hand for the shadow on the wall.

Why can't we screw this up?

Because we've already lost damn near everything to our tolerance. Taleb spotlights how kosher and halal foods muscled in on flexible groups, and that example unlocks it all. Over the last few decades, we've watched the inflexible clinch victory with the wedge of religious chow. They first claim an ironclad bind (their desert god bars them from unblessed grub), then leverage that to make their demand non-negotiable. From there, they've already won, because they dump the adaptation burden square on the tolerant pack.

The tolerant bunch sees its bendiness as smarts. By chasing props for such "smarts," it plunges into a trap it built itself: It thinks it's outshining the so-called "radical" Right, the one it scorns and figures it's slapping down with the label, but really it's just folding to Lefty demands.

Which never yields an inch, schooled as it is in intolerance's muscle.

On the flip side, this flaunted tolerance crumbles the second ego's on the line. That's exactly what our YouTuber demos at his video's close: After puffing open-mindedness as his edge over my "narrow brain," he bids anyone who wants to spill on his channel to fuel future podcasts, before tacking on an "except you, Timothé" that guts his open-minded pose in three words.

This contradiction, equal parts funny and revealing, outs the shakiness of declarative hot air. It echoes a core truth Rousseau nailed: Our virtues always bow to personal gain.

Proclaiming tolerance is a breeze; living it against a status threat? Not so much.

So let's clock that the Left seized its turf through ruthless steel, not bendy give-and-take. The Left doesn't do "open-mindedness."

By betting on fake virtues, this digital Right dooms itself to style-over-substance purgatory. It mistakes moral coziness for real power, the kind that remakes the world. Online, where ideas slug it out with no holds barred, indulgence isn't virtue, it's a luxury for gorgeous losers.

A brutal way to polish the superego while the foe slides pieces across the real-world board.

3. The Right's Non-Racism

By folding racism into intellectual downgrade, a thought-collapse, and a moral foul, the values Right, desperate for a thumbs-up, over-rates its brainpower and gulps down the poison the Left meant to slip it.

But swigging the serpent's venom, the bite you dread, wasn't exactly the sharpest play.

The ban on Whites eyeing themselves, weighing their own worth, identifying with their group, celebrating it, and ultimately Preferring it, was precisely the lock we had to smash.

Bottom line, the real question we must face is this: Can Whites normalize White in-group space again?

Like before Europe's invasion.

Faced with that, this YouTuber opens his video cool-as-ice: "Me, I've got nothing against it."

That mild-mannered blandness even snapped me out of my daze. It takes real poise to tackle the gravest crisis hitting White societies, the outright ban on us Preferring ourselves, with such dialed-back restraint.

But deeper in his video, he drops a grave, vengeful zinger: "You've lost an ally," his way of bailing on the White Identitarian cause because yours truly dared critique him.

I don't know what grown man ditches a cause he allied with over a mere slight, but this bat strategy, aimed at pleasing two crowds, the Identitarians and the sovereigntists, pushed me to craft the full take-down here.[1]

We're living in an era where a former Supreme Allied Commander of NATO forces, General Wesley Clark, declared in 1999 during the NATO intervention in Kosovo: "There is no place in modern Europe for ethnically pure states. It's a nineteenth-century idea,

---

1   The bat strategy means flashing "look at my wings" to birds, and "check my fur" to mice, to whisper "I'm one of you" no matter the audience.

and we're trying to transition it toward the twenty-first century. It is through promoting multi-ethnic states that we are doing that."

A head of state announced he'd wield the republic's tools to reach the supreme goal of miscegenation. We can't play lukewarm or flip-floppy on this. Whites own Europe, and they must rule it. Or they'll fade from the continent that's theirs.

In truth, it's often a war of tone, of shaking off inhibitions, of probing mindsets, pitting us against our invaders. More than a clash of arguments that only sway us. Our invaders see us as pushovers because we still fear our own "racist" rage. It strikes us as morally ugly, like an aikido practitioner finds a raw right hook crude, ugly, something he's never learned to throw, yet it packs a hundred times the punch of his fancy moves.

If the Right-wing channel you're subbed to online hasn't nudged you one inch toward this Preferist uninhibition, unsubscribe.

Why does inhibition define the whole sovereigntist sphere? It's a business model. Hook the attention of Whites sensing a massive identity crunch looming over their fate, then hold them with a fog of sundry hot topics that water down the identity core. Then cap it by slamming the heart of the fix, tumbling back into the left's big taboo "racism," that word weaponized to criminalize Whites' right to Prefer.

This YouTuber, who crowed about dodging the racist Right label, has probably snapped out of it by now, I hope. But the non-racist vibe still soaks the analytical rRght's mental bath. It's the poster child for that cautious line viewing us as lowbrow extremists, funneled into cartoon radicalism, all the while as it casts itself as the grown-up, thoughtful, presentable Right. The fact that I show my face while this YouTuber (and so many others) hides behind a kiddie plush avatar should make him rethink that.

Bruised by 50 years of the Left's stinging charges, especially of brain-dead stupidity, this values Right craves to flip the script and become the accuser camp.

Figuring it can make the Left its prey, it piles on fascism and racism jabs, books clean-cut Arab guests for its shows, and disowns the Preferist tractor that could yank it from the ditch.

"Too good for you," it sneers at us, dolling up for the ball like a stolen truck.

But neither the modern Left nor its old-school kin will dance with you. From Soral to Rougeyron, nothing's shifted. What the Right itself dubs "racism," whose core is Preferring, still gets eyed not as a fix, but as a lesser evil than the Left claims.

The racism charge is like a net flung at a foe: if it doesn't spread, it stays balled up and useless. And that spread hinges on media relay, gripped by the Left.

As long as the sovereigntist Right keeps playing by the enemy's rules, it'll lose via self-racism. The art of smart alliances means ditching hoary grudges. The Identitarian White in the frontline trench isn't the rival to envy; he's the only ally on deck.

If you're aiming at the foe from the rear trench of Right-wing non-racism, you'll end up shooting in the back of what you claim to guard.

4. A Deadly Seriousness

The sovereigntist Right rarely turns its followers into charmers. Like a mother blind to the nuances of allure, it drills the men who follow her to be dullards. Always solemn, relentlessly analytical, it's a tough sell to snag attention in a crowd with that baggage. Laughter and fun have swung hard toward the Preferist right.

"So yeah, I'm probably racist. You asking that to hook me up with your sister?"

It's this breeziness, this hedonistic edge, that could unburden them from the slog of dreary intellectualism, the sort bogging down a Right swollen with endless navel-gazing.

The plague of centrist hot takes already sours the national mood enough. Do we really need to heap more bricks on that wretched knapsack?

The testimony from that center-Right kid, which I took the liberty of ripping, fit the bill: gutsy, granted, kind-hearted, I know the type (I was that kid once too), but so cowed by everything he ought to revolt against, and above all, profoundly disheartening.

Our YouTuber, for his part, spelled out that "we, the three-digit IQ set," must dissect our subjects from every angle to grasp every shade.

But the opposite holds true: Analysis now just buys time at a standoff, we already hold all the cards. What's the crisis, who's the foe, who's overrunning us, and how webs of communities plus natalism can shape the counterpunch.

That these brainstorms never spit out anything beyond the next dissection should set off sirens. The internet Right has morphed into a sitcom. And that's no fluke.

This "analytical farce" is its own blueprint, fueling the economic grind of these players, none of whom earn personal venom. But the revenue model riding that infinite analysis carousel has hardened into the snag. This Right (and I'm not zeroing in on this YouTuber) genuinely thinks the probing's just warming up. Often raised without a dad, it pays the price of no direct download: It grabs core truths only via books or vids, breeding the fantasy that nothing's been nailed down yet.

Prepping the next breakdown, that's the gritty core of their blueprint. But reality's blueprint runs a different script.

Nations quit supplying identity long ago, and the culture scrap's over. Whites scatter from a Third World hunkering down and seething at us (a grudge we could hurl back tenfold, if influencers fanned disinhibition instead of pasteurizing everything with overthink).

Legitimizing Preference for Whites outweighs fretting if pierced woke drama queens can be salvaged. But I get it's a steeper bet on arenas like YouTube.

And as always, the Right's crowd shoulders the first blame for what it hypes, and thus nurtures.

5. Diluting the Value of What Matters

To wrap up by broadening the lens, I want to flag a crucial split that's jumped out since Covid exploded the creator pool, audiences, and output: the gap between what's interesting and what's important. This isn't some minor tweak, it's a bedrock rule. It hits Preferist content as hard as sovereigntist Right-wing stuff. I'm throwing this at myself as much as the Right-wing sphere: It's one of our biggest time sinks.

Online, the interesting explodes; the important fades. We can geek out on endless topics. None of them matter.

The boundless opinion flood has birthed a frantic video junkie, while we starve for real clout around our ideas. Plenty of creators' raw honesty makes critique a minefield, read as spite or envy. Still, urgency doesn't vanish with slicker talk; it just worsens when we water it down.

Thousands of testimonies and books stack up like stray sparks, but the riposte blaze won't catch. The fuel's splashed on wet ground. Entertainment neuters anger. Overload of info and breakdown feeds our brains the fake-out of progress. Since the '80s, the chant's been: "One day, it'll blow! Can't last forever!" As clocked, nothing's blown. That no-show blast soothes: It green-lights kicking action down the road, mixing up interesting and important cheapens action.

I'm not saying every call to move is gold. But infotainment runs alongside action without really fueling it. The interesting swells and struts. The important bows out and retreats. How do we flip the script?

The blueprint of a methodical White Freemasonry, building brick by human brick from its talent pool, still lacks steady grind. The conservative scene does spark meetups, hookups, some upsides; but more by happenstance than dogged method, shaping passions, and that Trotskyist-grade seriousness in the fight.

Without that, anti-White hate won't turn into spur, conquest, or power grab.

I've tinkered with pitches to shift from infotainment to action plans. Any influencer grabbing identity for clicks should commit to foundation-laying turf: stuff that swells real community networks' ranks, that amps their social muscle, clout, and cash flow.

No rival crew skips goals or ends.

"The Turkish family means at least three to five kids per woman," Erdoğan recalled in March 2017.

That's marching orders, not chit-chat.

The analytical tone and urge to map the mess don't tip into action. Notoriety must morph into command: prescribe, set timelines, track dashboards. Crowds get riled. They don't act. We need to hit them in David Ogilvy, Gary Halbert, Dan Kennedy, or Christian Godefroy's lingo, the copywriting greats, the bridge to doing.

We need a borrowed-time ethic from subs: what attention toll do I charge them?

What do they lose if this content vanished?

What clear, measurable goal do I chase, by when? Where's the hard call to action at the end?

No Identitarian channel should claim endless airtime. Time's the resource we can least afford to burn. The 21st century's likely our big sieve.

The street-mic case spotlights this nicely. I'd snag it to unpack Vincent Lapierre's work, a standout in the game, and emotionally sharper than the YouTuber I figure I've answered. By handing the mic to street folks in these trottoirs, Lapierre logs real pluralism. He bets our era's move is letting people hash it out. But here's the snag.

Not only does airing opinions just mirror the lazy thought ruts we all nurse as hobbyists, it also brews a fake unity in the gripe-fests that's killer at the polls. Since it rarely gels into vote unity. Dissidence wallows in polling when it should prescribe: steer, dictate, make necessity's musts (priorities, budgets, timelines) a moral lock, instead of stacking one more sample.

Folks craving hierarchy and parasite-idea purges get nudged to churn more takes, instantly hoovered by a machine that pretties and spices them for fresh commentary, layering opinion on opinion.

While we drown in word soup, free speech turns into hobby. A sidestep.

What should hog our focus, building ops networks (mutual aid, funding, skills, local roots), and shove news to the back burner. The game is not tallying views, but herding elites of execution around sharp, shared targets.

Course, Calendar, Cash-in.

If content skips a course, sets no calendar, says zilch on deliverables, it entertains.

Important doesn't shine by shouting. It shines by changing.

Less noise, more works.

White Eschatology

SINCE THE end of the First World War, Whites seem to have lost interest, little by little, in their genetics and its transmission. They have grown ever more passionate about ideologies and modes of thought, altruism, liberalism, Orientalism, communism, spirituality, economics. Learned diversions carry them off into the sky of ideas. These speak to them of everything except their blood and send back a flattering image of their intelligence. Being White has become an awkward footnote in their identity, they are flesh that wants to become a concept, sometimes flesh that only wants to mutate, to get beyond the body in any case. We should not blame them for this, nor even judge them. We should understand them and make them another offer, a better offer, one that can harness their desire for elsewhere, carry them along, and still save their genetic future.

That offer may be contained in the idea of a rational eschatology. Let us try to sketch its outline. If a racial vessel carries through the ages the specific aptitudes of our genetic family, can we imagine that one aptitude in particular might end up becoming a superpower and play a decisive role, the power to cancel the destructive leverage our environment has over us? Eschatology has until now meant a discourse on the end of days. The scenarios told by the monotheisms all end that way. That is what gives them unmatched sacrificial power, an absolute goal and a meaning no one dares to contest.

What happens, though, when people begin to understand that the end promised in the holy books risks being, like the beginning, a mere allegory? Someone pointed out to me recently that on board the *Titanic* people prayed for God to warn human beings of flesh and blood and hasten the arrival of help. No one prayed for the ship to be carried through the air to New York harbor, a thing Abraham surely would have asked for. That clear case of rationality lodged in the heart of modern faith is telling. We are less and less inclined to believe in order to save the world, because people sense that if the world is to be saved, it will be by human means. But which humans, precisely, will end up doing it for real?

It is a fact that if a major asteroid risk showed up in our telescopes, a risk that will arrive mathematically sooner or later, no one on earth would turn to Algeria, Rwanda, Palestine, or Haiti to kindle hope. This is not even about financial means, it is first about cognitive ones. A handful of Whites would bear the ultimate responsibility for directing such a project. The whole planet knows it or senses it. Disaster films from before 2010 merely illustrate this raw fact unconsciously. Whether you hate it or accept it, we would be practically alone at the controls in the face of a cosmic threat. "Don't look up," or you will see the White man once again.

The human group that built aqueducts and paved roads and drew maps is roughly the same as the one that explored the world, then launched the first satellites and reached the Moon, the same that is considering colonizing Mars, can scan the far reaches of space and send messages there, or set into equations the probability of extraterrestrial life, the same that also uses its genius to invent excuses for populations relentlessly prone to crime, whatever their social conditions. Even in the anti-racist theater you find tireless, and sometimes absurd, White creativity.

Dare we then inaugurate an era of rational eschatologies, ones in which the ultimate role of each human genetic group can be inferred from its history and its achievements? It is now possible to draw up the résumé of every people and to assess its ability to help save the world in the event of a large scale catastrophe. The point is not to infer any superiority, we live in the age of nonjudgment, remember, but a specificity. A nuance.

It is true, the idea of a European racial vessel sketches an eschatology that is delicate to assume, the idea that behind our role as the planet's kind nurses we are in reality the Promethean people, chosen not by an imaginary entity but by the record of facts. That is the last role today's Whites would like to assign themselves. Yet Promethean only has meaning within the community that produced the concept. For peoples that mishear it, it can look like arrogance. It is on them to grasp its sense better, for in truth it is only a responsibility. Vaccines, earthquake anticipation, storm prediction, early cancer detection, asteroid monitoring, flood control levees, forecasting the risks tied to artificial intelligence, pollutant management, attention to ecological shifts — the list is long of mortal dangers that have been reduced, sometimes very sharply, by man of European origin.

This variety of human may be the one most aware of the value of human consciousness as well as one of those that cares the most about others. These words may be hard to bear for billions of people on this planet, and harder still for a majority of Whites long accustomed to belittling themselves. But if the dwindling of Whites on earth continues, we will have striking proof that this was not just a theory. Despite our capacities as planetary superpredators, we cultivate and constantly heighten our compassion across the living world. Horrors persist, of course, yet it is Whites who find them most horrifying. One day, a vital share of animal species may owe their survival only to our ecological sense.

This description can sound presumptuous and even border on naïve supremacism, since we are used to looking with deference and dread at Nature's immeasurable destructive power and to viewing with shame, sometimes with rage, the technological traces we leave in this world, traces that cannot, obviously, all be positive. The posture I recommend does not deny the negativity necessarily brought by White progress and innovation. It simply means setting our recent technological victories back into the long arc of time, where we can chart as accurately as possible the value of our technological creativity and what it says about our "cosmic role."

Must we keep cultivating that awed dread of nature, and that shame at our technological prowess? Those two foolish emotions actually go hand in hand and invite us to remain in a kind of religious stupor. Nature is in fact a "neutral enemy" that will destroy us without meaning to, with all the stupid indolence of a boulder rolling down a mountainside above a village. That boulder is out there somewhere, hidden in the mountain of events in preparation.

Relentlessly reducing nature's destructive power could become our eschatology. Turning a hostile environment into the most perfect habitat is our specialty, and it will likely become so at the cosmic scale if enough time passes. We will not see a Dyson sphere or anything close to it in our lifetime, yet we know some of our descendants will inexorably keep probing that idea. To be blunt, the existence of gods is a cultural fiction from our ancestors' imagination, yet it could collide with the reality of our evolution. We are already gods compared with our distant forebears. Extend the curve of technological evolution based on our progress over the last two millennia by another two millennia, and what term would best describe our status then?

To switch tracks and thus change our fate, we must take off our costume as planetary nurses and take seriously our Promethean eschatology. An eschatology that plunges a people into one and the same quest, setting its children on that course, is probably the most powerful thought on earth for producing a common mentality and perseverance. Perhaps what we lack is a shared belief of high intensity. Other peoples dig their historical furrow and make their own torrent in it, using tales that are absurd yet gripping. A destiny that is gripping and realistic could surely achieve at least as much.

Only a shared eschatology lets us count ourselves, unite, and move forward in earnest. Only that lever lets us grasp the manifest rivalry of peoples with one another, harder to spot than a secret, a plain fact. Without the goal of a final destiny, and even without the prospect of a cosmic role, our racial vessel could drift indefinitely or assign itself a sacrificial role, for it burns with the unavowable feeling of being from another world.

If a rational eschatology is possible, then it will be the eternal 1% that must adhere to it with religious conviction. You've seen it: the mass eventually absorbs, it never initiates. To help us pivot into that kind of thinking, there is this choice: Become the servants of the hostile world that is rising, or become its gods, without judgment, never any judgment of course.

Every community might in the end be nothing more than an incubator. Ours, at any rate, cannot afford to steer its children toward roles too disconnected from our rational eschatology. Taking that seriously will necessarily outrage the common sense of the spectator society. It is impossible not to be a scandal when you confess such an ambition. Our children must hear stories in which the ultimate mastery of genetics, of deep space, and of designing ultimate robots is ours, and they must stand at the center of those stories so that they grasp them as prophecies. That will be our secret, our plain truth.

Political Paganism

I WISH HERE to initiate reflection on another reason, less overt yet fundamental, that compels me to invoke Prometheism and to credit it as the wellspring capable of igniting what I term Legitimate Preference. This concept would remain incomplete without opening a window onto the subtly "religious" dimension of Legitimate Preference itself.

Contrary to what Jef Costello believed, I hold no faith in some cosmic consciousness of which we might serve as emissaries. Though we emerge from nature's weave, it reaps no gain from our presence, nor are we the universe awakening to its own reflection.

Yet, for all that we amount to a mere contingency in nature's vast design, I deem the triad of intelligence, consciousness, and memory to possess a value surpassing all inert matter.

I harbor genuine respect for William Pierce, but my proposal does not merge with his. Any impression to the contrary may stem from my own imprecise phrasing, for which I apologize to any reader who drew such a parallel.

I am profoundly Pagan and rationalist, a disposition that inevitably shapes my thoughts, my anticipations, and my writings. It affords me the chance to elucidate what Paganism might signify in concrete terms, beyond the folkloric excesses that fancy themselves revivals of ancient forms.

The hypothesis I must lay before you as a prelude to my argument is this: Ancient European Paganism does not spring from our forebears' imagination, but from their memory. Bare invention proves inadequate to religiously synchronize tribes often at odds, scattered across so expansive a terrain. A mere poetic fabrication could scarcely yield pantheons as intricately linked and coherent as those recurring in Indo-European mythologies, where divine figures grow so akin as to become interchangeable.

The shared Indo-European roots, the parallel mythological structures (such as the tripartite functional schema identified by Dumézil), the recurrent motifs (gods in quest of hidden lore, artisan deities, sovereign gods), and the alignments across pantheons all attest to this broad common ground.

I contend that what birthed these traditions arose not from collective fancy or individual whims, but from the memory of humankind. In this view, the gods of our ancestral pantheons would be flesh-and-blood men who once trod this earth, deified in their lifetime or through the haze of ages.

If the gods of our Pagan pantheons amount to nothing more than actual forebears, exalted across succeeding generations' tales, then we must reevaluate these timeless archetypes.

Who were these ancestors elevated to divinity? Were they the inaugural kings who imprinted the tribal psyche amid the shift to settlement? War heroes, perhaps? Cannibal sovereigns, as Allan Arsmann posits in his series *The Bible Read by an Asperger's*, or else prodigies in their fields, wielding awe or dread to command fealty?

I cannot resolve this with certainty. But I am persuaded that our distant past harbors tangible human realities, rather than pure mythology, realities that largely elude us still. The ethereal, spiritualist lens of New Age neo-Paganism stands utterly alien to what once endured.

That time might transmute these recollections into metaphysical beings comes as no surprise. As early as the 8th century before our era, Greco-Roman statuary may well have amplified this conquest of the collective imagination.

This line of thought, whatever its merits, has nonetheless inspired the peculiar notion I seek to convey in this brief chapter: a new Paganism, or a Pagan new testament, which would invert the temporal axis binding ancestors and descendants.

Rather than unwittingly deifying the illustrious shades of a submerged past, this new Paganism would consecrate our progeny. From that pivot, the gods of the emergent Paganism become the transfigured heirs, the emergent figures we exalt to sanctity even now.

This reversal of time's arrow would also render the White future retroactive. It implies that our collective tomorrow as Whites must reverberate into our today, rather than dwindle into insignificance. Should it take hold, the grandchildren of our grandchildren might one day inquire of their fathers: "Tell me, Father, is it true that once upon a time, Whites were forbidden to tend their own destiny?"

More crucially, this outlook stands in radical opposition to the sacrificial societies that corrode our age. A sacrificial society is one that could countenance the martyrdom of little Ebba Åkerlund, the 11-year-old Swedish girl cut down in the 2017 attack, only to see her grave desecrated over 20 times, as if her memory were mere refuse to befoul.

It is the society that enabled the slaughter of young Lola Daviet, the 12-year-old French girl tortured and murdered in Paris in 2022, amid an indifference that chills to the marrow. This sacrificial society is one that profanes our descendants, strips them of sanctity, delivers them to barbarism beneath the stunned gaze of a civilization that appears to have forgotten the very essence of "protection."

"Sacrificial." The word itself evokes ancient rites of first fruits, where superstitious peoples proffered their firstborn to a tyrannical deity, Baal, of whom Yahweh may represent a shameful repression, in hopes of quelling wrath or bartering favor. Our modern societies, for all their polished veneer, have relapsed into this millennial vice, but with a more insidious hypocrisy.

They no longer immolate in the name of a bearded god or stone totem, but for abstract idols: "live together," "diversity," zealous egalitarianism. These fresh divinities demand their flesh tribute, our children, our heirs, our futures twisted into "no future," and we tender them, frozen by dread of judgment or an apathy that bows the spine. Each sordid incident, each desecration, each conspiratorial hush becomes an oblation on the altar of this contemporary creed, a faith that has lost all sense of the sacred.

The new Paganism I advance upends this necrotic logic. By sanctifying our descendants, by raising them today to the estate of the sacred, we shatter the sacrificial cycle. We refuse to feed them to ideals that scorn them. Instead, we render them beacons, transfigured icons that steer our choices and struggles. If our children are tomorrow's gods, then every deed, every resolve must erect a bulwark for their tomorrow, an arrow loosed toward their eminence. No longer does the past bind us; the future summons, a White future, retroactive, where Legitimate Preference evolves into a living prayer, a vow etched in the marble of our resolve.

Envision a world where our descendants might declare of us: "They knew how to Prefer us."

Admittedly, this redefines the divine, trading some wonder for greater tangibility. Yet it marks no diminishment. Nor must a Christian White forsake anything to embrace this fresh iteration of Paganism.

By granting our descendants the dignity of potential divinity through mastery of nature, we inaugurate a novel religiosity, unprecedented in its concreteness: One that hallows the time ahead.

Is this feasible? Can such a vision gain traction?

I would not stake my faith on it, were we not already en route.

Scientific projections today hold that children born after 2015 might endure beyond two centuries. We are literally talking about rendering death elective.

What could claim divinity if not such an attainment? I reiterate: This rendering of the divine diverges from what Christian Whites conceive, whom I, of course, esteem without reservation.

But there you have it, my Paganism in essence.

This outlook impels me to regard our Racial Ship's future not as abstraction, but as territory to safeguard, an extension of our whole being, once we muster the awareness.

I share this not from mere whim, but from conviction. Any paradigm-shifting vision that redirects our bearings toward tomorrow inevitably provokes backlash. Which does not suit my strategic aims.

The apathy of Whites toward their collective tomorrow appears tethered to their failure to project beyond themselves, beyond their own lifespan.

Typically, faith in an afterlife shoulders that burden, resolving it through narrative and pledge.

At least when such projection into eternity still stirs the imagination.

But high-IQ Whites have largely abandoned assorted creeds. The rest believe in fits and starts. It has become a reasonable faith, policed by good sense. A faith that credits the hereafter yet prefers to defer any firsthand reckoning as long as possible, and rightly so.

The radical Muslim retorts that he cherishes death as the Westerner cherishes life, and therein lies his strength.

He has scented this frailty, as a shark scents wounded prey from miles off.

Against the rise of "the world's dumbest religion," to borrow Houellebecq's phrase once more, we cling to New Age fluff and "faith in humanity."

As fitting as draping a curtain against a charging rhinoceros. I suspect we shall require a profound counterforce to Islam, one rational yet rallying to unite Whites against the radicalized Third World's anti-White surge.

Nietzsche speaks truth when he urges contemplation of our collective life's immortality to blunt death's paralyzing sting.

Islam arms its warriors morally with afterlife conviction.

Must Whites resort to the same ploy to rearm?

Such a wager leaves me unsatisfied, given the arc of the hyper-technological societies now encircling us.

It is not a matter of undermining Christianity while it endures, but the momentum unleashed by AI's dawn will ineluctably reshape our beliefs in unforeseeable ways, at least beyond my powers of foresight.

If Prometheus, in Greek myth, dared seize fire from the gods to bestow upon men, then modern Prometheism must reverse the gesture: to wrest from men and bequeath to tomorrow's gods, that is, select descendants, the terms of transcendent existence.

Nostalgia finds no quarter henceforth, only Preference exalted to its apex.

An ethic of the future, a religion of the lineage.

The 15 Rules

Deyr fé,
deyja frændr,
deyr sjálfr it sama;
en orðstírr
deyr aldregi,
hveim er sér góðan getr.

Cattle shall die,
Kindred shall fade,
And thou thyself shalt perish;
yet fair fame
never shall fall,
for he who hath won a noble name.

Deyr fé,
deyja frændr,
deyr sjálfr it sama;
ek veit einn,
at aldregi deyr:
dómr um dauðan hvern.

Cattle shall die,
Kindred shall fade,
And thou thyself shalt perish;
but one thing I know
that never shall die:
the judgment on every man's deeds.

— *Hávamál*

Introduction

WHITES READY to practice the politics of Legitimate Preference form an active minority within a minority of conscious Whites. Everything suggests that, despite current events, Whites will not switch en masse to racial realism. They will do so drop by drop. Becoming such a minority will likely plunge us into a crisis. A crisis that has already begun. It will feel like an irreversible catastrophe. And indeed, **becoming** a minority is a terrible pain. But **being** a minority is not necessarily so. The paradox only makes sense once you've lived it. Not only is it not a disadvantage if the minority is active, organized, and determined, it may even be our only chance to reverse the situation. Freed from the moral duty of easing the misery of the world, forced to face our own ancestral singularity, can we finally focus on the sole interest of our own people and our descendants?

History shows that organized minorities often set the course of society. For that, we need three qualities:

Intolerance. Opportunism. Clannishness.

Not tolerating what reduces our collective happiness. Seizing whatever offers an advantage to our kin. Reserving for them alone our individual genius, our virtues, and our capacity for action. These are the three tools needed to overturn unfavorable situations and give our genetic vessel an edge. Ordinary morality usually treats these three qualities as grave defects. But morality that seeks its own principle for its own sake, in the Kantian way, misses the point. What we want is to increase the total stock of happiness within our genetic family. That means all the states that expand what our bodies and minds can do. Everything that serves that end is our morality. The morality of **Storge**. We call it our **Common Good**. And everything else must be abandoned.

To unite an enlightened minority, having a common enemy is neither sufficient nor even necessary. What we must do is synchronize our efforts and globalize, as fast as possible, this Western Bushido that follows in the rules ahead, all dedicated to the morality of Storge. To grasp the spirit of these 15 rules is to grasp that they are not profane. Cultivating these virtues, without giving up our free time, must absorb our energy so fully that none is left for opposing aims.

Every member of the Preferist family must favor, for himself and then for his kin, the creation of harmonious White households whenever circumstances allow.

A harmonious White household is the basic cell where our identity can grow free of outside interference. Once upon a time, certain women played the role of matchmakers; that precious role must be revived, if only to spare us the wasted time, the romantic missteps, and the suffering that come with searching blindly for a reliable partner.

Parents, too, once influenced the choice of spouse. That ancient role must be updated and adapted to modern life. What we have gained in freedom of choice, we have lost in years squandered discovering everything on our own. Elites who send their children to the *grandes écoles* know full well how vital it is to spare their offspring that wasted time.

We must also distinguish between the ascending family, our parents and ancestors, to whom we owe our very existence, and the descending family—our children and their children, to whom we owe loyalty. It is the defense of their interests that proves whether our devotion is alive or misdirected. The boomer generation often exemplifies what it means to neglect one's descendants.

Preference for our kin must outweigh every other sympathy we may feel for outsiders.

If a non-White neighbor asks for help while my cousin struggles to make ends meet, the choice is obvious. But the real rivalry in a White man's mind is not between kinship and charity, it is between Preference and meritocracy. Especially when immediate economic concerns push you toward pragmatism.

Do you hire the experienced Black worker who needs no training—or the young White graduate just entering the workforce?

An impatient gardener planting an orchard can choose an already grown tree, sturdy but near the end of its fruit-bearing years, or a fragile young sapling that will one day feed generations.

The Preferist choice is an investment made with a long-term mindset, not a short-term transaction.

And above all this: the Preferist cause must always appear as an **interest**. Anything perceived merely as a virtue will always lose out to the defense of an interest.

Meritocracy is best understood as a fragile virtue, a hope of instant reward tied to immaturity. Preserving the White in-group must be seen as a solid interest, an act of maturity.

Show only one face within the Preferist community, and reserve cunning for the outside world when necessary.

Social conventions demand masks from everyone. But that mask must never deceive our own, never corrode intra-community trust. A Preferist who lies to his kin betrays Storge and hands arguments to universalism by inviting self-serving comparisons between the bad elements of our community and the good elements of non-Whites.

On a stay in Oslo, after a hospital visit, I found no payment desk — only an open box at the entrance where patients left their due. Walking out without paying would have been easy, but the idea never even crossed my mind. That level of trust — now impossible in my own country thanks to Third World immigration — reminded me how precious and fragile it is. It flows from a specifically White cultural trait: the ability to internalize responsibility and guilt as tools of social regulation.

We must preserve and strengthen that capital of trust, without extending it beyond our community. This principle does not call for gratuitously cheating outsiders. It calls for absolute loyalty to our kin. Neuroscience and cognitive science show clearly that human empathy is limited, shaped by evolutionary mechanisms that favor in-group cooperation and out-group suspicion.

Our enemies thrive on our internal divisions, but they fear our cohesion. Imagine their dismay if that cohesion became an exclusively intra-community force, cultivated rigorously and sealed off from outside influence.

My kin are as precious as I am, though none of them is my strict equal. Each can either lift me up or be lifted by me. To accept this joyfully and to act on it is the driving force of a White group.

Every Preferist is a unique value within our rhizome. I advocate a living, dynamic hierarchy, where each rises or falls according to his abilities and his consistency in the Preferist cause, without illusions about himself, and without needless self-deprecation.

Keeping a flexible ego within the community is a form of mental hygiene. *"Maybe I was wrong"* is a phrase to keep close at hand in many situations, without lapsing into self-disparagement when exchanging arguments. This inner balance allows one to grow without arrogance and to assert oneself without rigidity, thus securing a strong and harmonious community.

The bond between Europeans of the past, present, and future must be the subject of regular meditation. Our individual consciousness is but a fragmentary expression of a supra-personal Promethean will, and our thought must remain tied to that idea.

In the face of death, most humans take refuge in belief. But there is another form of consolation: to see our existence extended in the lives of our descendants and their descendants in turn. They will live experiences that prolong our own, and they will think thoughts that we already thought, but otherwise.

This continuity is not some imagined immortality. It is real immortality. Don't just agree with the idea if it convinces you, dedicate time to it, let it steep in you. The human mind is like hot water in which you drop a handful of medicinal herbs. Replace idle or harmful considerations with this thought: your real life is supra-personal. It is the life that flows through you, not the one you temporarily borrow.

Begin each day with the fervent wish that our community remain happy, flourishing, and safe from harm.

This rule is simple. That is its difficulty. Many intellectualize life to such a degree that a morning ritual seems trivial to them.

And yet, a single thought or whispered phrase for the Common Good of Whites could dispel a great share of the negativity found on the Right's social networks. The constant, daily wish that our children laugh in safe schools, that our entrepreneurs succeed, that couples form, that our influencers prosper, that our elder Preferists stay healthy—this alone would destroy much of the jealousy and petty quarrels that eat at us.

This simple effort, once you know a hundred others are doing it at the same time, makes you realize you share something with those hundred people.

Be cordial. Be empathetic. Forget your kin's small faults. Put your harshness aside and offer kindness to one White every day. In this eighth rule, Legitimate Preference shines a hundred times brighter than in any scholarly discourse.

Each of us must train to renounce hostile rivalry and to practice useful rivalry instead.

Rivalries within a White society are either useful to the common good or harmful to its pursuit. A functional White society is made up of circles of sympathy that recognize and channel positive rivalry within themselves.

This rule is not a moral precept in the sense of opposing an instinct. It does not deny rivalry, it simply seeks to channel it. Male rivalry is a stubborn fact as long as hormones exist. The aim is to push hostility as far outside the White endogroup as possible, leaving only rivalry that is useful. This is a high ideal, but it lies within everyone's reach.

Our ancestors built empires by channeling their rivalries, not by drowning in them. This effort must be practiced at the intra-community level, but it must never be extended into that abstraction called universalism. The great mistake of modern Westerners has been to extend sympathy indefinitely to the global level, thereby diluting the natural bonds of solidarity.

That is not a moral elevation. It is psychological disorientation, an evolutionary short-circuit that leads only to fragmentation and collective inefficiency.

Create the conditions for prodigy to come. Prometheism is the common effort to increase the power and the overall happiness of the lineages to come. It implies a cult of health, of the body, of knowledge, and of positive eugenics.

Imagine our descendants tackling challenges that now seem beyond our reach, thanks to a strong and healthy generation we ourselves shaped. It begins with concrete choices: a Preferist striving for a diploma, another taking up sport again after illness, another helping his kin with studies, another creating edifying stories for White children. Each one cultivates that prodigy.

Health is not vanity, but a gift to future generations. Knowledge is a weapon for their conquests. Positive eugenics, such as encouraging fertile and harmonious unions, is not a taboo but a vital necessity. Without this effort, our grandchildren will inherit an empty shell.

Our enemies are betting on our physical and mental decline. That single "detail" is reason enough to cultivate the opposite. Prometheism is our challenge to natural entropy and to human hostility.

Reserve our genius for our own kin.

This ninth rule is above all a mindset, perhaps the hardest to make heard. Who would dare, in an age lulled by the myth of universal knowledge, to proclaim that we must keep our treasures for our sons? And yet, it is a truth that no one denies in secret. Generals do not share their battle plans. Engineers guard their patents. Why should medicine, art, and science be sacrificed on the altar of "humanity" as if offered up like virgins?

The truth is harsh: knowledge is not equal for all. The powerful heal their children with remedies the poor cannot even imagine. So what do we choose? To lift up our own, Whites left behind, or to throw our pearls before a world that spits in our face?

Take history as a mirror. Our vaccines, the fruit of Western genius, saved millions of lives. But they also triggered the demographic explosion now overwhelming us. That is not an accusation. It is a fact.

Universalism, that naïve dream, drowns our brilliance in an ocean of ingratitude. Algeria, which we built and handed over to enemies, taught us that generosity without return breeds hatred, not gratitude.

Our ancestors did not build libraries for the world, but for their children. Why should we do less? Let us reserve the lion's share of our knowledge, won through sweat and sacrifice, for our schools, our hospitals, our households. Let our genius inspire envy rather than jealous hatred.

We are now living through the collapse of the opposite model, and its bitter fruits poison us: hatred hurled at the White hand that tried to save the world.

Become a model for the anti-Preferists, especially the youngest, by confronting them with our unapologetic Preference.

Creating opinion shifts among our opponents, cracking their certainties from an early age, and seizing war trophies (converting White individuals to Preferism) from the "anti-Preferist" camp is the best asymmetric war we can wage.

A Preferist who lives his identity without shame, celebrating his heritage publicly, can fascinate a young soul lost in self-denial. We can weaken the opposing dogma by example, simply by being more attractive than the average personalities of everyday life.

We should keep a tally of converts, of White brothers brought back to the fold. This war is not won by argument, but by the living example that shatters their illusions.

Our enemies count on the apathy of future generations. But we can pull some of them out of their hibernation, then a few more, then others still. I dream of an endless razzia among the youth of the Left.

A charismatic Preferist role model is a torch in their moral night. This is how we reverse the tide, one mind at a time, each taking his turn.

Seek out social roles that allow you to advantage Preferist communities, and direct personal fortunes toward the emergence of Preferist content in culture.

Securing influential positions actively deprives ethno-masochist Whites of the benefits of their self-hatred. Our efforts must aim to disadvantage self-hating Whites who drag us down collectively.

A Preferist who becomes a journalist can slip in narratives valorizing our heritage. A fortune invested in a film or a Preferist school shapes minds. These roles are not privileges; they are levers to put an end to White self-flagellation.

An employer who hires his own defies the dominant narrative. Self-hating Whites actively sap White morale; countering their influence is a duty. Without this strategy, culture remains a hostile swamp. This is our silent reconquest of minds.

The function of Conservation (Tradition) within Preferist society is to serve Progress.

Any progress, material or immaterial, that deserves to endure because of the moral or material improvement it brings, becomes de facto a tradition.

Preserving an ancestral rite, such as a harvest festival, is not nostalgia but a reminder and concrete image of past progress, won by the first settlers.

The way we understand conservation must turn toward producing modern traditions that reshape our vision of technology, filtering out the simulacra of "Progress" from what truly gives us an advantage.

Reduce the gap between scientific discovery and understanding of the world.

The more our understanding of the world aligns with scientific knowledge, the more we keep up with the state of research, the more active we can be in the face of nature. Scientific illiteracy now carries a cost too high for us to bear as a group.

Without synthesizing current knowledge and assuming the duty of a high level of general culture, we remain socially dominated and at the mercy of beliefs and pseudo-sciences that drag us back. This principle also ties in to the loss of chance caused by false knowledge.

Our ancestors shed their false beliefs by observing, testing, and experimenting. That is the path they traced, and we must walk it.

A Preferist who informs himself about current research in neuroscience is a better disciple of the adage "Know thyself" than a purely literary philosopher. He will go further still if he can explain the existence of races against those who deny them.

We should all be able to explain to a child how our genes carry our specific traits and make tangible our unity.

Pass on to your children a stimulating metaphysics, one that evokes our ancestors and sanctifies our descendants.

Whatever your beliefs, whatever you tell your children to explain your worldview, make sure they feel carried by a genealogy and called by an attractive destiny.

We all have a universe of spiritual or intellectual references, but it must give our descendants confidence that they are not like the others.

Tell them that all their ancestors had to traverse time so that they could be born. Tell them that each ancestor desires their greatest success, and that no one will accomplish what they are about to accomplish.

Above all, tell them that their descendants will be even more prodigious still.

Each Preferist community must pool financial resources in order to maintain a treasury dedicated to promotion, assistance, support, reward, and an emergency reserve for members of their community.

As long as the State has not been reclaimed by Preferential logic and put at the service of Preferist society, contributions will be distributed illegitimately.

It is structurally necessary to have our own funds while awaiting the reconquest of the State apparatus. In France, the militant Left literally lives on a mountain of money and, thanks to it, manages to launder its image in the media despite the mountain of evidence of its anti-White hatred.

Possessing a war chest is a necessity for twisting the narrative in our favor. Truth by itself has no power. Storytelling has it instead.

As I write these lines, Marxist influencers, heavily financed by their supporters, repeat that "there is no such thing as native French, because several European tribes came to France a thousand years ago." They have been saying this for 40 years, and will keep saying it for 40 more.

They know reality is not discovered, it is fabricated, it is twisted. And we, defenders of White identity — who among us wishes to become a "twister of reality"?

Who will build that war chest if not you?

END

Metapolitical Glossary

Preferism: A doctrine affirming the moral, political, and anthropological right to prefer one's own without justification. It does not rank, hierarchize, or judge: it prefers. It is a method of symbolic survival adapted to societies where judgment is forbidden but action must remain possible.

Preferist: One who adheres to the philosophy of preference. He does not seek to convince, he seeks to live according to his preferences without asking permission.

Detradition: A concept designating the systematic destruction or severing of a tradition, its forms, its mediations, and its effects on reality. A word coined to account for phenomena of radical secularization and cultural uprooting.

Reinfusion: A metapolitical process aimed at reinjecting meaning, values, and narratives into a field emptied of its traditional significations. It is the Preferist response to detradition.

Adopter's Syndrome: The behavior by which an indigenous majority adopts the mental, cultural, and affective categories of the minority or incoming group, to the point of wanting "to be part of it." A psychological variant of Stockholm syndrome.

Plane of Immanence: A term borrowed from Deleuze designating the contemporary ideological framework in which all verticality (order, hierarchy, authority) dissolves in favor of a horizontal world. In this plane, everything is equivalent and every strong affirmation becomes suspect.

Emotional Block: A set of conditioned affective reactions that prevent the expression or logical analysis of a social or ethno-political fact. This block is activated by keywords, symbols, or media figures (e.g., "racism," "living together").

Majority-Minority: A statistical minority within a given space that nonetheless wields symbolic power or institutional authority equivalent to that of a majority group (e.g., NGOs, ethnic groups protected by law).

Verbal Counterfeit Money: A concept designating words redefined or diverted by an ideological camp to capture the collective imagination (e.g., the word "racism," diverted so as to have only one target: the White man).

OTHER BOOKS PUBLISHED BY ARKTOS

OTHER BOOKS PUBLISHED BY ARKTOS

OTHER BOOKS PUBLISHED BY ARKTOS

OTHER BOOKS PUBLISHED BY ARKTOS

www.ingramcontent.com/pod-product-compliance
Lightning Source LLC
Chambersburg PA
CBHW021621270326
41931CB00008B/808